T0146995

POWER 365

POWER IN THE WORD, POWER IN THE NAME, POWER IN THE BLOOD

*Power in the Word–Learning to
Trust & Surrender to God!*

*Power in the Name of Jesus—Learning
to Trust Oneself after Surrender!*

*Power in the Blood—Learning
to Embrace the Present!*

Dr. Janie Sheeley Torain

POWER 365
POWER IN THE WORD, POWER IN THE
NAME, POWER IN THE BLOOD

Scriptures referenced are taken from the Blue Letter Bible King James Version online at http://web.ccbce.com/multimedia/BLB/ index.html unless otherwise noted in the footnotes.

Other sources referenced in the footnotes.

Given the transient nature of online publications, it is possible a web address may no longer be active or may have been altered since the print date of this book.

iUniverse books may be ordered through booksellers or by contacting:

iUniverse
1663 Liberty Drive
Bloomington, IN 47403
www.iuniverse.com
1-800-Authors (1-800-288-4677)

ISBN: 978-1-5320-5896-7 (sc)
ISBN: 978-1-5320-5897-4 (e)

Library of Congress Control Number: 2018912027

Print information available on the last page.

iUniverse rev. date: 10/08/2018

Table of Contents

Introduction

It had to be the Power of God's spoken word that allowed a share cropper with no education and nine children to instill in his middle child, the author of this book, the thirst for knowledge and the desire to be a lifelong learner. Power according to the thesaurus is the same as authority, control, rule, influence, and supremacy. As the people of God exercise the power given to us, we become authoritative, commanding, influential, controlling, and prevailing—other words powerful people of God!

My dad would always speak to us using these words, "If you learn how to read, you can go anywhere you want to go and do just about anything you want to do". He would rebuke anyone else that tried to speak anything negative over us. Words are the most POWERFUL entity in creation! Proverbs 6:1-2 says,"[1] Thou art snared with the words of thy mouth". Proverb 18:21[2] and says, "Death and life *are* in the power of the tongue: and they that love it shall eat the fruit thereof."

Dad's prayers and words of encouragement thrust me to be the first of his children to graduate high school and become the first generation college graduate. I received an Associate in Applied Science (AAS) in Accounting and Business Administration. I transferred to a four year university and received my Bachelors of Science (BS) in Business Education

---

[1] https://www.blueletterbible.org/kjv/pro/6/1/s_634001

[2] http://web.ccbce.com/multimedia/BLB/index.html

within two years. During my teaching career, I returned to college to earn a Master of Arts (MA) in Education Technology; an Educational Specialist (Ed.S.) degree in Curriculum and Instruction; and a Doctorate degree (Ed.D.) in Educational Leadership.

During my studies at the Christian university from where I received my doctorate degree, I experienced the Power of God through a "Divine Connection". Seventy-five percent of my classes were online, do I needed connection to the internet. The college was a two hour drive away. I literally received an internet connection that was named "Divine Connection". This was after finding out that no local companies provided internet connection in the rural area in which I lived. The "Divine Connection" lasted four years, until I finished my studies and then it went away as suddenly as it had appeared!

I had the desire to write at an early age. I published my dissertation research, *Virtual Learning: Is It Conducive to Student Achievement*, and my master thesis, *An Assessment of the Impact of Technology on the Performance of Exceptional Children in Computer Adaptive Testing in Person County*. I have another Christian book, *A Quick Guide to the Personal Qualities of an Evangelist*. I have also written one children's book, *If I Could Quit School for a Day*. I serve my local church and community as an usher, choir member, and Evangelist and Sunday school teacher. God has given me the Power to Speak the Word of God from the pulpit on the second Sunday of each month.

Jesus **SPOKE** the world into existence with power. Take a look at the thirty-one verses of Genesis Chapter 1 and you will see "And God said. . .[3]" numerous times. Look a little farther in this same chapter and you will see that God gave us

---

[3] https://www.blueletterbible.org/kjv/gen/1/1/s_1001

dominion over all the earth. This dominion is the governing power or right of governing over all that is placed before us. This book provides you with power filled scriptures. Speak these scriptures of power over your life daily. Speak with power over your children, finances, co-workers, body, and all areas of your life

After God's resurrection, he told his disciples to go to Jerusalem and wait. Over in the book of Acts Chapter 1, Jesus told them that they would receive power after the Holy Ghost shall come upon them.[4] We, as Christians, need to learn about the Holy Spirit and allow him to move with **POWER** in our lives. The Holy Spirit will bring us joy like we never knew it before. Joy unspeakable!

The Holy Spirit has a personality and will not force anything on us, but as we open ourselves up to him, he will teach us, so we can get to know God and what his will for us is. We must allow, receive, and be obedient to the moving of the Holy Spirit. We learn the will of God by reading his word, the Bible, assembling ourselves with like believers, attending Bible studies and teachings, and listening to the preachers and five-fold ministers of the gospel. Then we must DO!

The Holy Spirit has gifts that he is ready and very willing to give to you, but we need to know what these gifts are and ask for them. These gifts are given for the edification of the church as spoken of in I Corinthians Chapter 14.[5] He also speaks of the gifts to the church in the book of Ephesians, "And he gave some apostles, and some prophets, and some evangelists . . . For the perfecting of the saints for the work of the ministry, for the edifying of the body of Christ."[6] As we prove our faithfulness to him he will give us more and more of his power and gifts.

---

[4] https://www.blueletterbible.org/kjv/act/1/13/t_conc_1019008

[5] https://www.blueletterbible.org/kjv/1co/14/1/t_conc_1076012

[6] https://www.blueletterbible.org/kjv/eph/4/11/s_1101011

The Holy Spirit guided all the authors of Scripture so that what they wrote was not only their own words but also the words of God himself. Each of them had their own personality, however, when it came to the truth of God's word, they heard from the same source. This is the way the Holy Spirit deals with us today. One will have an outgoing jovial personality, another a more conservative serious personality, and yet another a running, jumping, screaming personality, and still another a no nonsense, stand still and speak direct to the people. All these gifts must find their source from the same Holy Ghost.

When we depend on and trust in the Holy Spirit, we will walk in the power that Jesus went to the cross to allow us to have. "No prophecy was ever produced by the will of man, but men spoke from God as they were carried along by the Holy Spirit"[7]

Jesus promises his disciples that they would receive **POWER** when they received the Holy Spirit AND they will be His witnesses, going about boldly to tell the people of the miracles and good deeds that Jesus had done. That is why I do not understand any true believer that will not boldly proclaim that Jesus is Lord. A cowardly personality that conforms to whatever the world is doing is evidence that the Holy Spirit is non-existent in the professing believer.

God is not a man that he should tell a lie. It came to pass that later, when the disciples were "filled with the Holy Spirit"[8] they **SPOKE** the word of God with boldness. In addition, Paul's preaching to the Thessalonians resulted in many conversions because his preaching came to them not only in word, but also with **POWER** in the Holy Spirit and with full conviction. In addition to that, Paul was a living,

[7] https://www.ligonier.org/learn/devotionals/word-god-words-men/
[8] https://www.gotquestions.org/Spirit-filled.html

breathing example in his daily walk with God—That is what we must be as well!

In this book, you will find scripture statements that can encourage you throughout the year. Some days will have personal testimonies and many will have scripture statements for each section: Power in the Word, Power in the Name of Jesus and Power in the Blood.

The Word of God conceived in the heart, formed by the tongue, and spoken out of the mouth has **POWER** to live an abundant life! This book will provide you with **POWER** to endure 365 days every year. Look up the scriptures referenced in the book and study them. Ponder the power of God in the testimonies. Reminisce how God's power has been evident in your life. Share this book and your testimony with others.

Read this book from cover to cover, and then again to be lifted out of discouragement and depressed attitudes. Remember the daily scripture and say it over to yourself several times daily. Refer to the book of the Bible that the daily devotional was taken from. Read the entire chapter. Reference the scripture to other scripture that speaks to the same topic. Use the version of the Bible of your choice. I mainly use the King James Version (KJV), however, I have also referenced other versions to confirm my understanding.

Finally, immerse your mind with these creative words, dynamic testimonies, and life-changing thoughts. Slowly but surely this process will change YOU and in turn change your life and benefit those around you.

Acknowledgement

To God be the glory! God gets the honor and glory for providing me with a companion after God's own heart. Thank you, Nathaniel, for being the man of God that prays for me and supports me in all the endeavors in our 31 years of marriage. Thank you to the children, grandchildren, great grandchildren, sisters, brothers, co-workers, friends, family, love ones, and even my enemies that have allowed me to experience the true **POWER** of God!

God Loves You!

God wants a relationship with you. He made a way for us to find forgiveness and begin again. Start that relationship with him today! Power 365 will give you day by day encouragement to live by the Power of God through his Word which is — our daily food for survival.

Power in the Word of God–Learning to Trust & Surrender to God

When confronted with temptation from the devil, Jesus said, "It is written!"[9] Do you remember to do that when the enemy of your soul comes against you? Jesus told us that we should do greater things than he did. Do you trust him? Do you believe? Do you have a personal relationship with him?

It was the spoken Word that created everything. Therefore, it is so important for you to memorize and speak the Word. The Word is God. Make it a part of your everyday devotion. You don't have to remember every single word or verse perfectly, but you should be able to recite the word of God concerning who Jesus is, and what he did on the cross. Can you tell anyone about Jesus? After all, the gospel message is the most important message there is to tell anyone. It is the **POWER** of God to salvation for everyone who believes.[10] God's grace and mercy endures.

You may not have the confidence to speak the Word of God right now. Maybe you, like Moses, are not very eloquent in speaking. No worries. It is not an issue of confidence or eloquence. Instead, it's an issue of trust in God's Word. You keep meditating on the Word of God, speaking with boldness,

---

[9] https://www.blueletterbible.org/search/search.cfm?Criteria=it+is+written&t=KJV#s=s_primary_0_1

[10] http://web.ccbce.com/multimedia/BLB/index.html

memorizing and you will experience power. I want to share these testimonies with you. Consider what I say, and may God bless you.

Power to Speak to the Family

When we started dating, my spouse was a very shy man of few words. When I say shy, I mean to the point that the family would be holding a conversation, ask him what he thinks, and fifteen minutes later he would answer. No one would know what he was talking about because they would have gone on to four or five different topics since the question was asked. He would come to pick me up and would sit in the car too timid to come to the door. *(I did not make it any easier because I was not one of those girls that ran to a man. The man had to pursue me. Just for the record, at that time I wasn't saved either. Ladies, the Word say, "a man that finds a wife", that means that we ladies are not the ones looking.)* OK back to the testimony of my spouse.

He said the family talks so fast and too loudly that it took him a while to collect his thoughts. You see, it was 9 children in my family and 21 in his. He would say that by the time it got around to him saying something, everyone would have said everything that had come to his mind. He spoke enough and well enough that we were married about six years later. I wanted to give you that foundation to tell you of the power of the Holy Ghost.

My spouse was born under the denomination of holiness. In which, holiness is a way of life and not a denomination, but, that is an entire different story. I on the other hand was a party girl. He would go to church services and gospel music programs and I would go play bingo. However, I would ask him about the services and he would tell me scriptures and songs that were song. One day he finally told me to come and see.

Well I want to tell you those were the best words he could have said. I went with him to church and got hooked. The Word was the bait that caught this fish! Well you know the enemy of his soul was madder than fire. Now there is a husband and wife team he had to fight against.

Looking back, it seems that God told the enemy about my spouse the same thing he told him about Job. Have you considered my servant, Nathaniel? The enemy attacked my husband's mind and fed him the lie that no one loved him and that he would be better off dead. There were some great challenges that came about within the next two months until one-night Nathaniel tried to take his own life.

We had had a big argument, and he had driven off on the van. Around two o'clock that next morning, I heard the van pull back into the driveway. Still angry, I decided to let him stew in the vehicle. The Spirit of the Lord spoke to me to go get him. I started talking back saying, "I am not going to get him. He is the one that stormed off." I kid you not, the Spirit gruffly spoke again and pushed me at the same time. I ran to the van. I do not see how he could have driven the van home. The driver's seat was reclined all the way down to the point that he could not have seen the road to drive. The inside of the van looked demonic. He had tied the passenger side seatbelt around the door along with his sweater. There were every kind of over the counter medication you can name. The bottles, blister packs, and boxes all empty. I screamed at him, what have you done? I called for our daughter to help me get him out.

We both carried him into the living room. He was an ashy gray and cold as ice. The Spirit of the Lord told me to put him in his bed. Well, from the previous push and the shove, I knew I had better be obedient. Then I was guided to warm a blanket over the heat vent and wrap around his feet. When I did this, he began to throw up and gag. We then put him into my car and took him to the emergency room. They pumped his stomach because he told the doctors that he tried to kill himself by taking all the over the counter medication. They irrigated him using carbon.

He stayed in the hospital two days before being transported to a mental rehabilitation facility in another city. He stayed in the mental ward for two days before being released. The day he left, one of the nurses told him that he would be back. She quoted some statistics about suicidal people. He told her that he would be back to bring Bibles and to read and study the Bible with the residents.

He left that facility, called all the family members together, and told his story. He told of how the evil spirits were prompting him to go to different drug stores and purchase a much over counter medication that he could legally buy—extra strength. He took the medication with alcohol—he was not and is not a drinker. He told how the little imps were hopping all over the van and Satan was sitting on the passenger side telling him to tie up the door, so no one could get in and stop him. He said finally Satan told him to open the driver's door and once he did, all those little imps got inside of him. His spirit was taken out of his body and he was then taken to the pits of hell. He told of all the torment and seeing people that he knew. He said the pain in his stomach was unbearable. He told of seeing a little spot of light and his older brother was calling him. That's when he said JESUS!

The bright light became brighter and brighter. God took him around in the spirit and showed him all the people that loved him and would be devastated by his death. He was shown all the people that would not come to know Jesus if he should leave at this time and then he was back in his body.

Jesus told him how he would clean him up and how he was to be a witness for him to his family. At that time his mouth became super large and a huge ball of evil came out of him through his mouth. The medication, the imps, and all the evil that was in him. He said Jesus told him to go home, that your wife would receive him, and he was to tell his story. He told of feeling the van moving but he was not driving. He said that when I put the warm blanket on him, it was like an angle had warmed him all over.

Ever since the day he was released from the mental facility, he has been telling his story, pointing people to Jesus, and witnessing to his family and all that will listen. You see, his family and my family, knew without a shadow of a doubt that this had to be God! This was over 20 years ago. He serves as the chairman deacon of our church, choir member, youth Sunday school teacher, and preaches the word on third Sunday and whenever and wherever he is asked. The Holy Ghost makes the difference.

Do not allow the opinions of family, friends and/or coworkers and what they might think stop you from speaking the truth when an appropriate opportunity arises. Instead, let your concerns be more about what God thinks of you and let the powerful word of God accomplish what God desires. Remember, Isaiah 55:11[11] says that God's word will not come back empty without accomplishing what he desires.

Yield yourself to God to be an instrument of his Word, and in the process, watch how it changes others…as well as how it changes you.

---

[11] https://www.blueletterbible.org/kjv/isa/55/11/s_734011

Power in the Name of Jesus—Learning to Trust Oneself after Surrender!

A good name is to be chosen rather than great riches."[12] Jesus Christ has given Christians the right and authority to use his name. This means that Christians have been given the power of attorney. Legally, power of attorney is the authority to act on another person's behalf, at their request. It is authorization given by one-person (Jesus) permitting another (Christians) to act on his (Jesus Christ's) behalf. "And whatever you ask in my name, that I will do, that the Father may be glorified in the Son. If you ask anything in my name, I will do it."[13]

Power to Use the Name of Jesus in Everyday Life

One day my niece and I were shopping in a nearby city. We were planning on eating at this particular seafood restaurant but had passed by it and had to turn around on the four lanes in order to get back to the restaurant. Traffic was very heavy that day and when I pulled into the turning lane to go back left, I just vocally said, "traffic in the name of Jesus hold back".

---

[12] https://www.blueletterbible.org/kjv/pro/22/1/s_650001

[13] https://www.blueletterbible.org/kjv/jhn/14/13/s_1011013

Immediately the traffic came to a standstill and allowed me to make the turn and safely get to the restaurant.

She said, "Aunt Janie, how did you do that." My niece was amazed at the results that the name of Jesus had. I smiled and told her, "That's the kind of God I serve, and He is no respecter of person. He will do the same thing for you."

"Whatever you ask the Father in My name He will give you. Until now you have asked nothing in my name. Ask, and you will receive, that your joy may be full."[14]

The name of Jesus Christ is not a magic word. The power is not even in saying words, but in understanding and believing all that the name of Jesus Christ signifies.

Jesus' name represents:

- All His finished work on the cross
- Fulfilling God's plan of redemption and salvation
- Victory over sin
- Victory over death, and
- Victory over the devil's entire realm.

When the name of Jesus Christ is prayed, it carries all the power and distinction God gave to it. God raised Jesus from the dead, elevated him to His right hand, and gave Jesus a name above "every name that is named, not only in this age but also in that which is to come."[15]

---

[14] https://www.blueletterbible.org/kjv/jhn/16/23/s_1013023
[15] https://www.blueletterbible.org/kjv/eph/1/21/s_1098021

Power in the Name of Jesus for Healing

Nathaniel worked as an assembler at one of the home improvement stores in our home town. He was assembling a fan and was using a drill to put a hole into the metal that was to secure the fan. The drill slipped and went through his left thumb. He shouted out, "Jesus" and quickly put the drill in reverse. This caused all the skin, flesh, and thumb nail to come out with the drill bit. He said there was no blood and he quickly pushed all his skin, flesh, and thumb nail back in place, still calling on the name of Jesus.

God gave him to clean up the wound with alcohol (You know how alcohol burns.), but he had no pain. He got some liquid skin to put on the wound. Liquid skin or liquid bandage[16] is a topical skin treatment for minor cuts and sores that creates a polymeric layer which binds to the skin. It protects the wound by keeping dirt and germs out and keeping moisture in.

Today, if he did not tell you, you would not recognize that anything had happened to his thumb. He never lost the thumb nail, nor does he have a scar. His thumb healed completely in the name of Jesus!

Philippians declares, "God also has highly exalted him and given him the name which is above every name, that at the name of Jesus every knee should bow, of those in heaven, and of those on earth, and of those under the earth."[17]

Does the name of Jesus work every time? Wherever you have the free will of people with all the forces of evil readily at hand, I'll let you answer the question. You know that Jesus could not work any miracles because the people did not believe

---

[16] https://en.wikipedia.org/wiki/Liquid_bandage
[17] https://www.blueletterbible.org/kjv/phl/2/9/s_1105009

him and what he could do. Matthew, Mark, Luke, and John speak to Jesus saying that a prophet has no honor or is not accepted in his own country, in his own household, nor among his own kin.

They Don't "Know" Me?

I am from a family of nine children. Three boys and one girl older and three boys and one girl younger. That makes me the middle child and middle girl. My two older siblings were charged with the care of me when I was three years old. I walked off during their care and wondered to the tobacco fields where our parents were working. My two older siblings got reprimanded for their lack of attention to my care. The next time, they tied me to a tree before playing.

Fast forward to now. I am an accomplished professional. I have my own tax services. I am a business and adult basic skills teacher. I have my own tutoring service. I have several degrees: Associate in Accounting and Business Administration; Bachelor of Science in Business Education; Master of Arts in Educational Leadership; Educational Specialist in Curriculum and Instructions; and a Doctor of Education in Educational Leadership.

I am telling all of this to say that my older siblings still see me as that three-year old runaway that got them into trouble. My three-year old actions were their main conversation at our family gatherings until I finally confronted them. I asked one question: After all these 57 years, jobs, degrees, TV and newspaper articles; is this all that you can remember about me?

Hebrews states, regarding Jesus, "when He had by himself purged our sins, sat down at the right hand of the Majesty on high, having become so much better than the angels, as He has by inheritance obtained a more excellent name than they."[18]

On the day of Pentecost, the people were deeply moved after Peter's powerful sermon, and asked, "What do we do?" Peter answered, "Repent, and let every one of you be baptized in the *name of Jesus Christ* for the remission of sins; and you shall receive the gift of the Holy Spirit."[19]

One day Peter and John were going into the temple, when a lame man asked for a donation. Peter said, "Silver and gold I do not have, but what I do have I give you: In the *name of Jesus Christ* of Nazareth, rise up and walk."[20] Later, when interrogated about this healing miracle, Peter was bold in defending the name of Jesus and all it stands for. "Let it be known to you all, and to all the people of Israel, that by *the name of Jesus Christ* of Nazareth, whom you crucified, whom God raised from the dead, by him this man stands here before you whole. Nor is there salvation in any other, for there is no other name under heaven given among men by which we must be saved."[21]

It is by faith in this name above all names, the name of Jesus Christ, that people are saved, set free from bondage, healed of sicknesses and diseases, and made whole. There is no other name under heaven more powerful or more significant, and this is a dynamic reality that Christians can believe in and have complete confidence in.

[18] https://www.blueletterbible.org/kjv/heb/1/3/s_1134003
[19] https://www.blueletterbible.org/kjv/act/2/38/s_1020038
[20] https://www.blueletterbible.org/kjv/act/3/6/s_1021006
[21] https://www.blueletterbible.org/kjv/act/4/10/s_1022010

Power to be Healed from Diseases

Since the fall of man, humans have suffered all manner of sickness and diseases. Doctors, nurses, and other health care professionals have been given gifts to help mankind, but faith in the name of Jesus and what he has done still trumps all. Back in 1975, I had several lumps removed from my right breast. Glory be to God, the doctors determined that the lumps were not cancerous!

Thirty years later, I went in for a routine mammogram and the x-ray showed a lump in my right breast. A referral was made to the women's clinic in another city for a confirmation to be made before deciding as to what would take place next. At this time both my spouse and I have become true believers in God and determined to live the abundant life that Jesus had given us. In the parking lot at the women's clinic, my husband anointed me with oil and we prayed and agreed in Jesus' name that my body was healed. When the mammogram was taken, NO lump was found! Thank you, Jesus!

"These things I have written to you who believe in the name of the Son of God, that you may know that you have eternal life, and that you may continue to believe in the name of the Son of God."[22]

Again, I urge you to practice applying the scriptures in your life daily. Having faith and believing the power is good, but practical application, walking in that power, in everyday life is the best.

---

[22] https://www.blueletterbible.org/kjv/1jo/5/13/s_1164013

Power in the Blood of Jesus— Learning to Embrace the Present!

When I started attending a Holy church, I would always hear the church mothers pleading the blood of Jesus over everything and everybody. Being a farm girl and having seen the slaughter of animals, and all the blood, I recall thinking how gross! It was not until I got the boldness to read the Bible for myself and then ask questions of the mothers, that I understood the power in pleading the blood of Jesus.

You see, in the Bible, after the fall of mankind in the garden, I had read how the blood of the lambs, bulls, goats and other animals were sacrificed year after year for the remission of sins. There were even particular animals' blood for certain sins. There was also a precise way you had to prepare the animal and apply the blood. These animals' blood could never cleanse the sins of the people, which is why they had to come back year after year. Hebrews spoke of the priest standing in the temple daily offering the same sacrifices over and over, which could never take away the sins of the people.[23] Then along came Jesus!

To make one thing clear before we go any further—Jesus is God. John chapter 1 verse 1 says that the Word was in the beginning, that it was with God and that it was God. John goes on to say around the 14th verse of that same chapter that

---

[23] https://www.blueletterbible.org/kjv/heb/10/11/s_1143011

the Word became flesh and dwelt among us.[24] When you get a chance, read the entire chapter one of John. There is power in it.

Now let's get back to our conversation about the power in Jesus's blood. Revelation refers to Jesus as the "Lamb slain before the foundation of the world."[25] If you recall in the book of Exodus, Moses told the elders the procedure for preparing the Passover lamb before the day they were to leave Egypt. He told them to apply the blood on each side posts of the door and the upper door posts of the house where they were to eat the meat of the lamb. Exodus chapter 12 is some more good reading to get the full story of applying the blood. [26]

The same way there were specific instructions for the Israelites, the Bible holds specific application for us to experience the power in the blood of Jesus. Let us take time to understand the significance of the blood. The Bible tells us many powerful things that the blood of Jesus does when applied. As you gain power over your life, reading these day by day scriptures, you will learn that when you follow the appropriate procedure to apply the blood, it:

- Provides forgiveness sins.
- Allows life more abundantly.
- Brings you closer to God.
- Cleanses your conscience.
- Gives you boldness to approach God.
- Sanctifies you.
- Cleanses you.
- Heals you
- Enables you to overcome the devil and his works
- And many more blessings

[24] https://www.blueletterbible.org/kjv/heb/10/11/s_1143011
[25] https://www.blueletterbible.org/kjv/rev/13/8/s_1180008
[26] https://www.blueletterbible.org/kjv/heb/10/11/s_1143011

Does applying the blood of Jesus works every time? Well, I'll share three of my many testimonies with you and leave it at that.

Plead the Blood of Jesus for Thankfulness

On June 9, 2003, I got a frantic call from my daughter who was eight months pregnant with twin boys. She had gone in for a regular routine checkup and the doctor found only one heartbeat. She was scheduled for an emergency C-section but would not allow them to do anything until I got there. I was over 60 miles away which is over a 90-minute drive.

I started pleading the blood of Jesus over my daughter, the twins, the doctors, the traffic, the drivers, myself—you name it. When I arrived at the hospital about two hours later, I was prepped and directed to the delivery room. My daughter was alert and not as frantic as she had been when she called. She had been given an epidural anesthesia and talked during the whole procedure.

The doctor delivered the twin that did not have the heartbeat first. She gave him to an assistant who put him in an incubator and did not try to massage his heart. My daughter became frantic again when she did not hear a sound and the doctor returned to deliver the second. After delivering the second twin, his cry was music to our ears. This music turned to fingernails on a blackboard when we heard the cry stop and the doctor announced a code blue. You see the second twin had stopped breathing. The medical staff from the nursery intensive care unit (NICU) came and speedily carry away the second twin. Still no one ministered to the first twin. I was still pleading the blood of Jesus.

The second twin stayed in the NICU for 19 days. During this time, we held the memorial service for his brother my grandson. The doctors also allowed my daughter to be released from the hospital to attend the wedding of her brother where she was a beautiful maid-of-honor. On June 28, 2003, we brought home a miracle! Glory to God in the highest! Thank God for the blood of Jesus that helps us to be thankful!

Plead the Blood of Jesus for Strength

It is amazing how our blood is designed to transport waste and toxin from the body. My daughter had been on dialysis for about 10 months. Dialysis is a treatment that filters and purifies the blood using a machine. This helps keep the body in balance when the kidneys can't do their job. My daughter had been in and out of the hospital with the longest stay over a month in a doctor induced coma.

On November 15, 2013, around 5:00 in the morning, I got a call from my daughter's hospital room. She sounded chipper and wanted to know when we would be coming down. I told her a soon as we picked up the children from school. This is the second twin who is now 10 years old and his sister who is 8. Around 2:00 we got a phone call from the doctor saying to come as soon as possible for they had just resuscitated my daughter whose heart had stopped beating. Pleading the blood of Jesus, we picked up the grandchildren and headed to the hospital.

That was one of the longest rides. While in route we got another phone call from the nurses' station that said her heart had stopped again and the doctors were still working on her. When we arrived, we were taken to her room where they had prepared her for viewing. The spirit that God had given her was gone. I plead the blood of Jesus! My husband and granddaughter were devastated. My grandson asked the nurse for one of those machines that would shock her back to life. I plead the blood of Jesus! He turned to me and said, "Grandma, it looks like mama is just sleeping. All we need to do is call her and she will wake up!" I plead the blood of Jesus!

On November 20, 2013, we had one of the liveliest home going for my daughter that the funeral director had ever seen. She was laid to rest in the low ground at the church with her son, the first twin. God has strengthened us to continue to raise her two children. Thank God for the blood of Jesus that strengthens us!

During my daughter's illness, she had come to know God as Lord and Savior. There had been a change in her life and lifestyle. The blood of Jesus is designed spiritually, to remove the contaminant of sin from our lives, which without we would be like the Pharisees in Matthew 23:27[27], "full of dead men bones and all uncleanness". Glory to God for the blood of Jesus that purges sin to allow us to walk in the newness of life!

Plead the Blood of Jesus to Live and Declare

On August 4, 2015, I was scheduled to have total hip replacement surgery. I had been pleading the blood of Jesus along with my church family ever since the decision had been made to have the surgery. The surgery was scheduled for 6:00 in the morning. The doctors performed the procedure without a hitch. It took me longer than usual to recover because of the amount of anesthesia that was administered. They also gave me, this is my opinion, too much Percocet (a pain medication with a combination of acetaminophen and oxycodone).

That afternoon around 6:00 p.m., I started coming out from under the effects of the medication. I started

---

[27] https://www.blueletterbible.org/kjv/mat/23/27/s_952027

hallucinating. I could hear this evil voice calling my name. I plead the blood of Jesus! I thought I was dreaming. I spoke God's word with power:

- I shall not die, but live, and declare the works of the Lord. [28]
- For God hath not given us the spirit of fear; but of power, and of love, and of a sound mind. [29] And many more.

The night nurses told me the next morning that I had preached all night long and that they had heard more scripture coming out of my room than they had heard coming out of the pulpit at their church. I had not been dreaming! There is a song we sing call "Old Satan; the blood of Jesus is Against You"!

Does pleading the blood of Jesus works every time? I say it's better to apply it and not need it than to not have sense enough to realize that you can't walk this walk without it.

There is Power in the blood of Jesus!

Days 1-2-3-4: Power to Witness!

But ye shall receive power, after that the Holy Ghost is come upon you: and ye shall be witnesses unto me both in Jerusalem, and in all Judaea, and in Samaria, and unto the uttermost part of the earth.
- Acts 1:8. (KJV)[30]

---

[28] https://www.blueletterbible.org/kjv/psa/118/17/s_596017

[29] https://www.blueletterbible.org/kjv/2ti/1/7/s_1126007

[30] https://www.blueletterbible.org/kjv/act/1/6/s_1019006

The first day! It could be your first day of the week, month or year. What a wonderful blessing! It is the first day of my year. We have just spent last evening bringing in the New Year with prayer, worship, and praises! It has not always been that way. In times, past, I would be recovering from a hangover— Not good. I would be wondering whether or not I had a good time. Had I offended anyone?

Power to Witness to Co-Workers

I score for the National Board for Professional Teaching Standards organization and was assigned to a site in Baltimore, Maryland for two weeks. I stayed in a hotel in a small city on the out skirts of Baltimore called Laurel and would drive each day to the work site. Before each scoring assignment, I ask God to direct me to the site where I can bring him the most glory.

At this scoring site, I was led to invite one of my co-workers to ride to lunch with me. I always keep my gospel music going for inspiration. As we conversed, on our way to lunch listening to the music, the conversation transpired to the topic of God. She asked me what I believed. I was accustomed to people asking me what denomination I was, but not what I believe. I answered that I believed in Jesus, him crucified, rose on the third day, and sent back the Holy Ghost to keep us and help us live holy. I then in turn, asked her what she believed. She responded that she was a Jew and they believed in the Old Testament scriptures only. She saw Jesus as a great prophet and teacher, but they were still looking for the Messiah.

The Holy Ghost in me gave the questions to ask her concerning the Old Testament scriptures that spoke to the coming of the Messiah. In answering my questions, the "light bulb" came on! Her answers got so ridiculous that she said, "That doesn't even sound right. That doesn't make any sense to me now that I have said it." In responding to the questions, she concluded that she needed to study the New Testament scriptures to get a better understanding. God is so awesome!

Power to Witness to a Stranger!

Everywhere I go in work or play, I look for a place to worship with fellow believers. I was told that on Tuesday that a church in the intercity of Baltimore has Bible study and teaching on that day. When I got home from work, I looked up the address and printed out a Google map. Around 6:00, I started out to find the church. Having never driven in Baltimore, I got lost. It was a scary ordeal. The further I drove the trashier the streets became.

I finally saw a police car sitting at a service station and stopped to ask for directions. They told me that the church was three blocks back the way I had come. Being a country girl, I asked them for approximate miles and street names.

When I arrived at the church on a Tuesday night, there were approximately 1500 people in attendance! I forget what section and row I was in but a young woman with pink and purple hair, too much make-up (my opinion), and smelling bad came and set beside me. After the teaching, the Spirit led me to give her a hug and tell her that God loved her. She sobbed violently and went down during alter call to give her life to God!

It is not God's will that any should die, but all should come to know him. He wants to give us abundant life. Thank God for his grace and mercy, I now have the power through the help of the Holy Ghost to enjoy this life and live it more abundantly. This scripture is true! Seek to receive this power daily. God loves you and desire to come and live in you. He promises, I will never leave you or forsake you. You will be a witness for him.

People will see that something is different about you. Some people will love the difference, and some will want you to remain the same as them. Those are the ones that will ridicule and slander you. Remember God loves you. Keep seeking him.

Days 5-6-7-8: Power to Live Holy

But as many as received him, to them gave
he power to become the sons of God, even
to them that believe on his name:
- John 1:12 (KJV) [31]

I have the power of the Holy Ghost! Keep this in your mind as you go about your daily duties. Say this throughout your day: I am a child of God! I believe in what Jesus Christ did for me. He wrapped himself in flesh; was born through the Virgin Mary; took on our sins and infirmities; was crucified on the cross; was buried and rose on the third day; was received up into glory. Hallelujah! God, I thank you!

---

[31] https://www.blueletterbible.org/kjv/jhn/1/12/s_998012

From the Mouths of Babes

When I asked my grandson, what does he thinks it means to live holy, he replied, "Doing God's work when he tells you to and how he tells you to do it." He also added, "Go to church every day or at least every Sunday." I think he added the last statement just because he thought that is what I wanted to hear.

However, I liked his first statement. Many people do not know that to live holy is a lifestyle. You get accustomed to doing God's will even when you do not feel like it. It is daily asking God, "What will you have me to do today? Who will you have me to bless today? Who will you have me to give a word of encouragement?"

My grandson was born with a "little old man's spirit" That is what I and his mother would say. He was in the infant intensive care unit at the hospital for 19 days. During that time, we witness some strange occurrences as to his behavior and interactions with the doctors, nurses, and us.

To live holy is to be obedient to God's instruction in the Bible. Paul charged us to present our bodies a living sacrifice, holy and acceptable to God. This is what we supposed to do. Paul also tells us to renew our minds. Our natural way of thinking is carnal and selfish. We are to have the mind of Christ.

I believe he sent back the comforter which is the Holy Ghost to live in me. I believe! As I commit myself to God, I have power to resist the enemy of my soul and he will flee from me. I have power to be kind to those I meet today. I have the power to live a Holy life. I believe God loves me!

Days 9-10-11-12: Power to be Bold

*And Jesus came and spoke unto them, saying, all
power is given unto me in heaven and in earth.
- Matthew 28:18 (KJV)*[32]

Jesus has transferred that same power to you and me. That's wonderful! Know this today! Speak this today! The disciples ran and hid, fearing for their lives after Jesus pronounced "It is finished" on the cross. Their faith was gone or very weak and wavering. But Christ gave such convincing proofs of his resurrection and told them to go into Jerusalem and wait together. At the appointed time, God sent the comforter and it made their faith to become victorious over their doubts. After the power transfer.

To Boldly Go Where No Man Has Gone

This was one of the statements at the beginning of a popular television program that I use to watch back in the day. It came to mind when I study the scriptures concerning the disciples, that they received the Holy Ghost on the day of Pentecost.

Jesus told them that they would go to Jerusalem and throughout the world and **boldly** preach and teach the gospel; the good news. The mission then as it is for us today. Tell about the goodness of Jesus; charging them to repent and have faith and trust in Jesus; most of all discipline them in everything that he taught.

---

[32] https://www.blueletterbible.org/kjv/mat/28/18/s_957018

He now solemnly commissions his ministers to go forth among all nations. The life that we are to live and the salvation we are to preach, is a common salvation; whosoever will, let him come, and take the benefit; all are welcome to Christ Jesus.

You say, "I know I have the power of God". Keep a song in your spirit today. One of my favorites is "Everything is Moving by the Power of God". I often sing the lyrics to a song that says, "I refuse, I want let nobody steal my joy! There is also another song named He Turned It! Some of the lyrics say:

> *The devil thought he had me*
> *Thought that my life was over*
> *He thought by now I'd give up*
> *He thought I had no more*
> *But that's when someone greater*
> *Stepped in my situation*
> *My morning has now begun, because*
> *He turned it!*[33]

Find you a great song of encouragement to help boost the power in your life today.

Days 13-14-15: Power in the Grace of God

But not as the offence, so also is the free gift. For if through the offence of one many be dead, much more the grace of God, and the gift by grace, which is by one man, Jesus Christ, hath abounded unto many.
- Romans 5:15 (KJV)[34]

[33] Tye Tribbett https://www.azlyrics.com/lyrics/tyetribbett/heturn edit.html

[34] https://www.blueletterbible.org/kjv/rom/5/15/s_1051015

Theologians have developed a method of interpreting history that divides God's work and purposes toward mankind into different periods of time called dispensations. Some say there are seven some say there are nine. But for right now, Adam is said to be in the first dispensation of innocence—until they disobeyed. We are now in the dispensation of grace. Jesus shed his blood for us and took on our sins and infirmities. Our responsibility during the Dispensation of Grace is to believe in Jesus, the Son of God

Whenever you are reminded of Adam's disobedience that condemned the entire human race, remember Jesus and his actions. Use the power invested in you to give praises to the second "Adam" who took away the sins of the world.

Your Grace and Mercy

Satan is the accuser of the brethren. He will remind you of every wrong thing that you have done and why you might as well stop trying to live right. When that battle is going on in your mind, say out loud, ***"BUT GOD'S Grace and Mercy Has Changed That! Thanks for Reminding Me!"***

Grace is the unmerited favor of God. Grace is lovely. Grace is elegant. Grace is refined. Grace is polished. Grace is the undeserved beauty God gave us in the place of our ashes. Allow the grace of God through the Holy Ghost convict you to change. Conviction makes you aware of wrong doing, and it also points you to the right way. It helps you correct the wrongs. Praise God for his grace and mercy!

Not only did he make a way for us to be forgiven for the sin that we have done and did not commit, He made it possible for us to live an abundant, healthy, and holy life right now. Remember God loves you. God's grace and mercy has brought us through.

Days 16-17-18: Power unto Salvation

For I am not ashamed of the gospel of Christ: for it is the power of God unto salvation to everyone that believeth; to the Jew first, and to the Greek. - Romans 1:16 (KJV)[35]

Do you willingly let it be known that you serve God? When you hear conversation that leans toward criticizing Christians, calling them "saved folks" or talking about "holy rollers", do you join in or walk away? If you truly serve God, you WILL be lied on, cheated, talked about and mistreated. You WILL be rebuked, scorned, talked about sure as you're born! Don't be discouraged.

Talked About, But Not Ashamed!

I am veteran teacher—at the writing of this book, I am retired after 31 years of service. I still substitute about three days a week. All my students know that I am a believer in Jesus Christ. Some of them have mocked and poked fun at me. When they would walk past my classroom door, they would say things like, "Praise the Lord! Hallelujah! Thank you, Jesus!" laugh and keep going. Their motives may have meant evil, but I was blessed! What they said replaced the cuss

---

[35] https://www.blueletterbible.org/kjv/rom/1/16/s_1047016

words that usually came out of their mouths. It also pointed me out as a go to person for prayer and consolation.

Many times, my co-workers would come by my room for prayer. Students would stop by before a test for me to lay hands on them or anoint them and pray. Some of the students that mocked me even came by to be prayed for. It got to the point that some parents of the students would stop by my room for prayer during conferences or open house. As time went on, more of my co-workers got the boldness to let it be known that they loved the Lord as well. The last year before I retired, the CTE department would hold prayer by the gym before the start of the school day. Teachers from other departments AND some administrators would join-in. Never be ashamed of the gospel!

Be sure when you pray over your food that you do it boldly; not a silent headache prayer where you pinch your forehead and bow your head and say nothing that can be heard. On the other hand, do not be obnoxious, yelling loudly with long drawn out prayers just to be seen and heard. Be sincere and real with your words, attitude, and actions.

Long as you got King Jesus, you can overcome anything the enemy puts in your way. Do not be ashamed. Peter denied knowing Jesus when he got around the wrong crowd. But after receiving that Holy Ghost on the last day of Pentecost, Peter could boldly say that we will obey God rather than man! Don't be ashamed of the power that God has given you. If you are ashamed of him, He will be ashamed of you.

Days 19-20-21: Power to Pray

***Confess your faults one to another, and pray one
for another, that ye may be healed. The effectual
fervent prayer of a righteous man availed much***
-James 5:16 (KJV)[36]

Admitting that you have issues and challenges is the first step in receiving grace, mercy, and forgiveness. Pretending to be perfect and allowing the One that is perfect that is in you to help you are two different things. James is not saying tell all your faults and business to anybody that will listen.

He is saying admit the wrong, repent, and stop so you may be healed from lying, gossiping, being jealous and many other little foxes that make you sin sick. Be mindful to talk and receive counsel from godly friends, family and leaders. Pray for yourself and others that you are sharing with to receive understanding and strength to make a change.

Prayer is communicating with God. It is more than giving God a "to do list" of things that you want God to do for you. It is also more than a request or plea for something that God has already done.

Lord, help us to talk to you like the "true friend" that you are and be thankful to you for your answers—regardless of whether it is what we want to hear or not.

Days 22-23-24-25: Power to Persevere

***Finally my brethren be strong in the Lord
and in the power of his might.***
-Ephesians 6:10 (KJV) [37]

---

[36] https://www.blueletterbible.org/kjv/

[37] https://www.blueletterbible.org/kjv/

What is perseverance? Do you hang in there until you are sure that you have done all that is in your power? To persevere is to be determine or endure "through" a circumstance or challenge. It is usually something that you prefer not to do. It is the going through the valley to get to the mountain top.

Perseverance to Re-write Dissertation

In 2004, I enrolled in Liberty University and started working toward my Doctor of Education with a concentration in Curriculum and Instruction. The program was hybrid, which included hours online, VHS tapes, CDs and 24 credit hours face to face. I attended weekends and summers and completed the entire program by summer 2006. In the fall of 2006, the university changed my program to Educational Leadership which changed my requirements. Perseverance!

I had acquired enough hours to apply for the doctoral program and an Educational Specialist (Ed.S.) degree, so I applied for and received my Ed.S. Degree and acceptance as a doctoral candidate in 2007. However, the degree specified Educational Leadership as the concentration. All my paperwork still said curriculum and instruction was my concentration. Perseverance!

During 2007, I went through all the proper procedures to acquire my dissertation committee and present my research topic. Upon approval and tutelage from my dissertation chair, I started my research and writing my dissertation. During this time of research and writing, I had to maintain three credit hours of enrollment. Perseverance!

In July 2008, all happy with approval from my committee and chair, I went before the Dean of Education to present my findings for my topic. I was called before the Dean and my chair and told that my dissertation was a sham and that I was a disgrace to the School of Education. The Dean said that I should be arrested! He gave me the ultimatum to re-write the entire dissertation. My chair apologized to me. My spouse and daughter were devastated! They knew how hard I had worked and the sacrifices I had made. I on the other hand took my frustrations to God! Perseverance!

On July 13, 2009, I went before the Dean of Education and the Committee with a re-written 150 page dissertation, <u>Virtual Learning: Is it Conducive to Student Achievement?</u>[38] At the conclusion of my 15 minute presentation, the Dean of Education and the Committee all had tears in their eyes and welcomed me as "Dr. Torain! Glory be to God for Perseverance!

In a society that has gotten accustomed to instant gratification, to persevere takes the tenacity of the Holy Spirit that God gives you.

Use the power that Jesus has invested in you. Stand firm on the scriptures that you do know and understand. Never lean to your own opinion of hearsay. Seek the Lord.

Lord, I need you to help me to stand strong within me to handle the circumstances of today seem to become heavy for me. Let me handle issues one by one this day. And most of all—help me to be thankful

Days 26-27-28: Power to be Submissive

Let every soul be subject unto the higher
powers. For there is no power but of God:

---

[38] http://digitalcommons.liberty.edu/doctoral/168/

the powers that be are ordained of God.
-Romans 13:1 (KJV)[39]

Submission is not a dirty word. One way of looking at submission is the act of surrendering or being obedient to one that has higher authority or responsibility. Submission can also be coming subject to another person even if they do not have authority over you. It is a choice to allow or give in to the wishes of another. Submission is not a one-sided ordeal.

In other words, the Bible instructs wives to be submissive to husbands as they, the husbands, in turn love them with their all in all. Employees be submissive to their supervisors or bosses and they in turn treat them fairly. Children be submissive to parents and parents treat them with the respect due. One submissive to another especially to the Lord.

If each person works on their part of being submissive and take responsibility for their actions, God will be well pleased. Concentrate on what you can change and have power over—YOU

Pray that God help you to stand fast unmovable, submissive to His will.

This is the day to reflect on how you treat and respect the spirit of God that lives in you. Your soul wants what it wants. Lord, help me to please you this day. Help me to be mindful of the spirit that lives within me.

---

[39] https://www.blueletterbible.org/kjv/

Days 29-30-31-32-33: Power to be Renewed

For the word of God is quick, and powerful, and sharper than any two-edged sword, piercing even to the dividing asunder of soul and spirit, and of the joints and marrow, and is a discerner of the thoughts and intents of the heart.
-Hebrews 4:12 (KJV)[40]

Today allow God's word to penetrate the very core of your mind—the heart. Meditate on it. Let your mind be renewed. Get rid of the stinking thinking. Think on the many promises and benefits in serving God. Cast your cares on Jesus and trust him to do what he said he will do. Let the word do what it was sent to do. We are cleanse by the Word.

A True Makeover

I like looking at shows that do makeovers: of homes, restaurants, even of our bodies. It amazes me how mankind can take an old shack and make it look like a mansion. How she can take a 1956 rusted out car and restore it to mint condition. How she can take a frumpy house person, give them a pedicure and manicure, give them a classy hairdo, and take them on a shopping spree to coordinate professional outfits, and make them look like a top executive or CEO of a company.

The makeover candidate is only successful if they listen to and follow the suggestions of the people trying to help them improve their appearance. The same go for the Word of God. When we follow the instructions for us presented

---

[40] https://www.blueletterbible.org/kjv/

through the Word, we will see a new creature internally and then outwardly.

When you follow the instructions of scripture, it will renew your mind. To renew your mind is to get rid of the old way of thinking and get the mind of Christ. Romans 12:2 reminds us to not be conformed to this world but be transformed by the renewing of the mind.

When you are reading scripture, and feel convicted, repent and sincerely turn away from the behavior or habit that caused you to feel convicted-opportunity to re-evaluate and change. The deception of the enemy is to make you feel condemned—without hope. Let the word do its work and God can heal all wounds.

Days 34-35-36-37: Power to Believe

Now the birth of Jesus was on this wise. When as his mother Mary was espoused to Joseph, before they came together she was found with child of the Holy Ghost.
-Matthew 1:18 (KJV)[41]

To be honest, when I read the scriptures, I can't imagine the faith and trust it took for Joseph, the spouse of Mary, the mother of Jesus, to believe the situation that he found himself in. Have you ever had a time when believing God took more faith and trust than at other times? You must believe that he is a rewarder of those that diligently seek him. Don't ever stop seeking him for guidance.

---

[41] https://www.blueletterbible.org/kjv/

Do you believe Matthew 1:18? If yes, then:

- You must believe that God wrapped himself in flesh and
- Was born through the Virgin Mary.
- He had no sin, but took on ours and carried it to the cross.
- He was buried in a borrowed tomb
- He rose on the third day
- He is seated at the right hand of the father
- He sent back his comforter to sustain us until his return for us.

Can you believe that? If not, keep on searching the scriptures and praying to God for understanding.

That fleshly body shed blood and died for the remission of sin. He rose on the third day. He sent the comforter, Holy Spirit, back to lead us and guide us into all truth. Believe this!

Days 38-39-40: Power to Prosper

Then he that had received the five talents went and traded with the same, and made them other five talents - Matthew 25:15 (KJV)[42]

God has given us all the tools and knowledge we need to be successful and a benefit to society. Are you seeking him for guidance in how to use these tools? He wants us to thrive and enjoy good health while we are growing in grace and in knowledge of him. To serve God is joy, peace and love. In

---

[42] https://www.blueletterbible.org/kjv/

all your ways acknowledge that Jesus is the one that made it possible and gave you the favor for you to do what you do.

God does not give us gifts and talents to hide or keep secret from others. When he freely gives us good health, financial well-being, knowledge in a certain area, he wants us to be a blessing to his people and his kingdom. We are to praise his holy name and let the world know who we serve and believe.

Use your gifts and talents to glorify God. Lord, you have gifted me with many talents. Thank you! But Lord, who am I that you would allow me to exercise these gifts without repentance. Help me Lord to reach out to your people.

It is possible for us to neglect the gifts of God within our lives, but God did not give us these gifts to be neglected. He gave us these gifts to be used. And so, Paul's exhortation to Timothy, "Stir up that gift that is in you," begin to exercise it again.

By faith, help me to exercise again that gift of the Spirit that you have given me.

Help me to help them know you as their personal Savior. Help me to find the methods and the right words to say to guide and inspire to seek you in all things.

Days 41-42-43-44: Power to Give

Then the disciples, every man according to his ability, determined to send relief unto the brethren which dwelt in Judaea:
- Acts 11:29 (KJV) [43]

Giving is a discipline in which you must make a conscious effort to include it into your everyday life. You were born

---

[43] https://www.blueletterbible.org/kjv/

with a spirit of selfishness. No one had to teach you to want to keep all your cookies to yourself and not give one to your sibling. No one had to teach you to cling to your bag of potatoes chips and dare other children, even your younger siblings to touch them. However, your parents had to keep encouraging you to give your baby sister one or even give them some of what you had.

There are many ways that we give. Most people think of finances when you hear the word give. But, we can give of our time to provide a service. We give of our material things such as clothes, shoes, etc. We even give out kind words or an uplifting conservation.

Lord! Today let the words of my mouth be edifying to your glory. Thank you for allowing my words to comfort and encourage those who come in contact with me. Thank you, God, for what I have. I know that what you have for me it is for me. Help me Lord to receive your many benefits and keep my eyes off what others have.

Have you helped someone today? It is not too late. Each day be a blessing to those around you. Sometimes it is as simple as listening. Don't give your opinion, just listen. It may be holding the door for someone. Helping someone relieve a burden is one of the benefits of loving God and loving his people. Today help me to be a burden lifter.

Days 45-46-47: Power to be Victorious

According as his divine power has given us all things that pertain unto life and godliness, through the knowledge of him that hath called us to glory and virtue.
- II Peter 1:3 (KJV)[44]

---

[44] https://www.blueletterbible.org/kjv/

The song often rings in my spirit, "Victory is mine. Victory is mine. Victory today is mine. I told Satan to get thee behind. Victory today is mine." So many professing Christians are appearing to live defeated lives because of the lack of knowledge of applying the word to their life. Many can quote part of the scripture but leave off some crucial points that can mean the difference between victorious or defeated in life.

For example, many profession Christians are quick to tell you to "resist the devil and he will flee". But the first part of the instructions says, "Submit yourselves therefore to God" (James 4:3). After you have submitted to God, then you will have the power to resist the devil.

Lord, thank you for investing in us the ability to live a godly life. You have already provided for me what I need today to be victorious. Thank you for allowing me to become your child. Today, your virtue shine through me so you can get the glory.

Days 48-49-50-51: Power to be Wise

For the preaching of the cross is to them
that perish foolishness; but unto us which
are saved it is the power of God.
- I Corinthians 1:18 (KJV)[45]

For some reason, in a worldly view, to be wise is to believe in yourself. If you believe and trust in God, the intellectuals say that you check your brains at the church door.

---

[45] http://topverses.com/Bible/1%20Corinthians/1/18

Wise to Pray!

Nathaniel had worked for this company for 33 years. It was the biggest employer in the rural town that we live in. In 2004, management had called the workers together to announce that the plant would be closing within two weeks. After hearing the news, Nathaniel immediately told all co-workers that believe in the power of God to join him in prayer. Nathaniel was in the process of finishing paying child support for which he had about one more year of weekly payments.

After they prayed, they all went back to work. Nathaniel came home, and we prayed together with our church family. The very next week, the workers were called together again and was told that the plant would continue to operate. It is always wise to trust in the power of prayer. Glory be to God!

A year later, right after Nathaniel finished paying child support, management called the workers together again. This time they were told the plant would definitely shut down in six months. Management told the workers that all of their investments would be safe, and they should not close out their savings and profit sharing accounts.

Two days later, Nathaniel was walking through the plant and the Spirit spoke to him to get his investment in the company out. He began the process of completing forms and requesting his funds. Those co-workers that had seen the power of prayer in keeping the plant open, now followed Nathaniel in getting their money out too. Management tried to convince them not to get their money by telling them how much taxes would consume their investment. It did cost Nathaniel over $40,000 in taxes. However, those that left their money in received nothing. In October 2006, the plant closed permanently.

It is true that God uses the foolish things of this world to confound the wise. Just think about the last time a theologian made a big deal out of the simple biblical concept such as grace and mercy. Just believe and receive is what Jesus say. Theologians say you must do and ear to call yourself worthy.

The ones that are smart in this world and depend on their own craftiness consider your word as foolishness. Help me Lord to know how to go in and out among these types of people. They are still your children too. Help me to stay mindful

Days 52-53-54-55: Power to Get Wealth

Deuteronomy 8:18 But thou shalt remember the LORD thy God: for it is he that giveth thee power to get wealth, that he may establish his covenant which he swore unto thy fathers, as it is this day.[46]

Wealth is often times seen as prosperity or richness. Wealth is also seen as success or achievement. Some dictionaries even tells us that wealth is an abundance of valuable possessions or money. Why do we always think that wealth is money? Moses reminded the Israelites that it was God that gave them the power to get wealth so he could establish his promised covenant.

Although God gives us power to get wealth, don't put your hope in it. Proverbs 23:5 tells us not to even glance at riches for it will take wings and fly away. In other words wealth is here today and gone tomorrow. Proverbs 10 goes on to talk to us about the slacker causing poverty, but the diligent hand makes

---

[46] https://www.blueletterbible.org/kjv/

one rich. Mark 8 warns us that gaining wealth at the expense of our soul is unprofitable.

God wants us blessed to be a blessing. The Word has much to say about that power to get riches. But be careful. Timothy warns us that those that covet after wealth, strayed away from the faith, and opened the door for much sorrow in their lives.

God wants us to be balanced in five domains; Socially, Physically, Emotionally, Intellectually, and Financially. In his words, he tells us:

- To forsake not to assemble-social.
- To prosper and be in health-physical.
- To renew our minds-emotional
- To learn of him-intellectual
- To get wealth-financial

Lord we are all your children and you have given us different abilities. Lord help us to use the power you have given us to get wealth and be generous in our giving to help others.

Days 56-57-58-59: Power to be Content

Philippians 4:11. Not that I speak in respect of want: for I have learned, in whatsoever state I am, there with to be content.[47]

Lord, why aren't everyone excited about your grace and mercy? Why isn't your love received with enthusiasm by all? What can I do to be more effective in loving and living the word? Am I expecting too much? Am I doing my best Lord,

---

[47] https://www.blueletterbible.org/kjv/

and can I be content with that which I am doing? How do I know if I am doing enough?

I experience today a great opportunity to be content. It was the fall of the year and leaves are everywhere on the yard. We, my spouse and I, were using the leaf blowers to corral up the leaves from around the gazebo then vacuum them up with the lawnmower. Well, my spouse thought it would be a great idea to mulch the leaves into the yard instead of removing them. To me, it looked a mess. I could feel the disappointment raising it head. My spouse is one that does not like being told how to manage what he calls his territory—the yard. I took this issue to the Lord. I started thanking him for having a companion that would care to maintain the yard. As I was being thankful for what I had, a sense of peace came over me. As I looked up, he was vacuuming the yard.

Lord, today I needed the contentment that only you can give. Thank you!

Days 60-61-62-63: Power of a Sound Mind

II Timothy 1:7 - For God hath not given us the spirit of fear; but of power, and of love, and of a sound mind.[48]

Having a sound mind in the secular world means legally, having the capacity to think, reason, and understand for oneself.[49] Adults (for the Western world standard age of 18 for females, 21 for males), by nature, are considered in general to be in sound mind, but through certain circumstances can be rendered as being not in sound mind, due to intensive brain damage or other major incapacities. Now evidently, Paul had sensed the fear

---

[48] https://www.blueletterbible.org/kjv/

[49] http://www.businessdictionary.com/definition/sound-mind.html

Timothy had of Nero's gruesome and cruel persecution of the followers of Christ. This reminder that fear is not of God can be your basis for holding on and trusting God today.

Fear is the tool that Satan often uses to discourage our exercises of the gifts of the Spirit. The thoughts that "I don't know what people are going to think, you know, if I say that to them." We have this fear that many times restricts us from receiving the many blessings and benefits of serving God.

Even if your mind is tempted to surrender to fear, as was the case with Timothy, you can allow God's Word and the Holy Spirit to work in you to deliver, rescue, revive, and renew your mind. This means your rationale, logic, and emotions can be shielded from the illogically absurd, ridiculous, unfounded, and crazy thoughts that have tried to grip your mind in the past. [50] All you have to do is grab hold of God's Word and His Spirit.

But "God hasn't given us the spirit of fear;" …but the Spirit of power! Oh, thank God for a sound mind.

Days 64-65-66-67: Power to be Delivered

The angel of the LORD encampeth round about them that fear him, and delivereth them.
- Psalm 34:7 (KJV)[51]

Remember this—You have been set free—liberated. God makes use of the presence of the good spirited angles for the protection of his people from the malice and power of evil spirits. The holy angels are present every day more than we are aware of.

Angles are no more dignified than the regular person nor are they superior to us. The angels are constant working in

---

[50] https://renner.org/what-does-it-mean-to-have-a-sound-mind/
[51] https://www.blueletterbible.org/kjv/

heaven praising God, and are entitled to a constant rest and bliss there, -yet in obedience to God, and in love to God's people, they help us to be delivered.

They condescend to minister to the saints, and stand up for them against the powers of darkness. They not only visit them, but encamp round about them, acting for their good. They hold back the hands of the enemy when we don't even realize that we are in danger. Have you ever felt safe in the mist of chaos?

All the glory be to the God of the angels.

Days 68-69-70: Power to Praise

Save us, O LORD our God, and gather us from among the heathen, to give thanks unto thy holy name, and to triumph in thy praise.
-Psalm 106:92 (KJV)[52]

We have so much to praise God for! Our daily walk is a testimony to the Glory of God. The Bible is overflowing with examples of praises for the healing of bodies, raising from the dead, thwarting the plans of the enemy, and bringing people to a relationship with God. Jesus did this for you and me. He loves us. We must receive this gift. Many times, we say a free gift. It was not free. Jesus gave his life for our transgressions. We need to praise him for all that he has done.

When we come to acknowledge that above everything else, Jesus is worthy of our worship and praise, then we can make a lasting difference in our life. Make a decision today to fix your eyes on Jesus, and daily give him praise. You will find that no matter what's the circumstance or challenge, you will

---

[52] https://www.blueletterbible.org/kjv/psa/106/47/s_584047

suddenly realize that God has already begun to release the grip those struggles can have over us.

We know we ***should*** praise, but in reality, circumstances and challenges of day to day living, it becomes a sacrifice to offer praise. Today, bless the Lord or my soul. This verse comes from a Psalm of joyous praise, in which the writer rises from a thankful acknowledgment of personal blessings to a lively celebration of God's gracious attributes.

The power of praise ***CAN***:

- Open the door for God's power to be manifested; miracles
- Make the devil leave us alone (for a season)
- Get our focus on God and off self
- Help us realize our need for God
- Keep us from complaining
- Refreshes our spirit
- Open the door for more blessings

Praise God for all his benefits. Help us not to forget the gracious hand which preserved us in peace, and multiplied and enriched and strengthened us. Let us not vainly imagine, in the deceitfulness of our hearts that all these blessings were produced by some superior wisdom and virtue of our own. Thank you, Jesus, for all the benefits.

Day71-72-73: Power of Restoration

He restores my soul. He leads me in the
path of righteousness for his name sake.
- Psalm 23:3 (KJV)[53]

[53] https://www.blueletterbible.org/kjv/psa/23/4/s_501004

Adam, which included Eve, had a wonderful relationship with God. They would commune together in the garden with long walks. They had been given dominion over everything. This was until Adam (both of them) decided to be disobedient.

Our soul consists of our mind, our will and our emotions. The Bible say because man fell from the grace of God in the garden, we were born in sin and shaped in iniquity. Therefore, we have a need to be restored to our original relationship with God. In step Jesus!

Daily surrounded by evil, God restores our souls and sustains us in love. Out beyond the guidance that is necessary to keep our feet on the path of righteousness, we will be away from our enemies, but never away from our Shepherd, our Guide, and our Host.

For we shall dwell in the house of the Lord forever. This is eternal life!

Days 74-75-76-77: Power of Comfort

Isaiah 41:13 For I the LORD thy God will hold thy right hand, saying unto thee, Fear not; I will help thee.[54]

Today let this verse be conviction of unbelief, and comfort of believers, or for the conviction of those in sin, addicted to idolatry, as multitudes are, and the comfort of those that allow God to help them keep their integrity.

Let this verse provide both admonition and encouragement to us, admonition to keep ourselves from idols and encouragement to trust in God... God by the prophet shows the folly of those that worshipped idols, especially that thought their idols able to contest with him and control him.

---

[54] https://www.blueletterbible.org/kjv/

God encourages his faithful ones to trust in him, with an assurance that he would take their part against their enemies, make them victorious over them, and bring about a happy change of their undertakings.

Days 78-79-80-81: Power to be Courageous

> *Deuteronomy 31:6. Be strong and of a good courage, fear not, nor be afraid of them: for the LORD thy God, he it is that doth go with thee; he will not fail thee, nor forsake thee*[55]

Lord, thank you for being ever presence with me! Help me to remember that and be thankful. You do not give a spirit of fear. Thank you for your grace and mercy. Two things might encourage my hope of your continued guidance:

1. The victories I have already obtained over the enemy of my soul, from which I see both the power of God, that he could do what he had done, and
2. The purpose of God, which he will finish what he had begun to do in me and through me.

Glory be to God! No matter what anyone say or do, they cannot take the power of God or the love of God away from me. I have no intentions to give it away either.

Thank you, Jesus!

---

[55] https://www.blueletterbible.org/kjv/

Days 82-83-84-85: Power to find Refuge

I looked on my *right hand, and beheld, but*
there was *no man that would know me: refuge
failed me; no man cared for my soul.*
- Psalms 142:4 (KJV)[56]

It is sad not to know where to find refuge from problems that bear heavily at times—this is the lot of many people. It is even sadder to not realize that we are in trouble and need divine intervention. Many people seek out friends or associates that do not know what to do in their own lives.

Sometimes, of course, this feeling may be because of unconfessed sin, as when David lamented after his crime of adultery and murder. Outwardly silent, but inwardly roaring—that is the way it is when a believer tries to rationalize and hide his sin from God and man. The remedy in such a case is obvious: Acknowledge your sin, confess your transgressions, and repent before the Lord.

When the problem is not one of unconfessed sin, the Lord is always there to comfort and guide, if we ask him. Lord, I repent and ask you to help me today.

Thank you Lord for being my refuge in times of trouble.

Days 86-87-88-89: Power over Confrontation

*And no man was able to answer him a
word, neither durst any man from that day
forth ask him any more questions
- Matthew 22:46 (KJV) [57]*

---

[56] https://www.blueletterbible.org/kjv/
[57] https://www.blueletterbible.org/kjv/mat/22/46/s_951046

Lord, thank you for the power over confrontation! Help my unbelief. Is God sovereign? Will he override free will? Jesus was always confronted by the Sadducees and the Pharisees. These two groups of people believed in and looked to the (known to us today as the) Old Testament Scriptures for guidance and motivation but refused to believe that Jesus was the Messiah. Because of their lack of faith, the Sadducees and Pharisees were always trying to trap Jesus by trying to get him to speak against the Old Testament law.

Confrontation?

Have you ever been accused of doing something or not doing something? Confrontation is given the synonyms in the thesaurus as hostility, conflict, clash or battle. The enemy uses confrontation to get your focused on the drama instead of the real issues.

As a mom, grandma, spouse, and school teacher, just to name a few of my roles, I am often confronted. Can you relate to any of these?

- You didn't tell me that...
- You didn't teach me.
- Why can't I go to...?
- How come they can't ...
- Why can't I use my phone to call...?

I am so thankful for the example of Jesus. He is the epitome of how we should handle confrontation.

Jesus silenced both the Pharisees and Sadducees with one

single word from the Scriptures. To the Sadducees, the word was "am", indicating that Abraham was still living. To the Pharisees, the word was "Lord", proving that the Messiah was both human and divine, descended from David but also David's Lord.

Jesus' foundation for his responses was based in each case on the determinative authority of just one word in the Scriptures. For Christ the Scriptures were inerrant and of full and final authority, and they could not answer His claims without rejecting the Scriptures which they professed to believe.

I believe! Thank you God for power over confrontation!

Days 90-91-92-93: Power to Walk Not After the Flesh!

There is therefore now no condemnation to them which are in Christ Jesus, who walk not after the flesh, but after the Spirit - Romans 8:1 (KJV)[58].

Ever been on a diet? By the time you eat breakfast, your stomach is growling for a snack. Ever passed by the candy dish and just got to have that chocolate kiss? Ever sit on the sofa all day watching movie after movie, when you know the clothes need washing, the yard needs mowing, and the house needs cleaning? These are the temptations of the flesh!

What does it mean to walk after the Spirit? Paul said, follow me as I follow Christ. Was Paul walking after the Spirit? Yes! God wrapped himself in the flesh and walked among us to be that example. We don't have to struggle and strive in our own strength. We must believe and receive the Spirit of God.

---

[58] https://www.blueletterbible.org/kjv/

There is no shortcut to learning how to walk with the Spirit. It's not just for ultra-spiritual people nor is it reserved for charismatic Christians. Life, walking after the Spirit is not simply trying to do the right thing, nor is it trying to live after God's Law. Walking in the Spirit is the central metaphor for describing what it means to live as a Christian.

Meditate on scripture. Take every opportunity to put into practice going about doing the will of God. The person who walks after the Spirit will in fact have the essence of the Law fulfilled in his life.

God is good. Any situation you find yourself in today, let nothing condemn you concerning serving Jesus. Lord! Help me this day to keep my mind on the sincere meat of your word. Keep me with the joy and peace you promised.

Days 94-95-96-97: Power to be Confident

> *Being confident of this very thing, that he*
> *which hath begun a good work in you will*
> *perform it until the day of Jesus Christ*
> *- Philippians 1:6 (KJV)*[59]

Confidence according to the thesaurus, is the same as trust, belief, and faith. It is the feeling or belief that you can firmly rely on someone or something. Many parents instill positive values in their children which in turn gave them the confidence that they could do anything or become successful in life.

Confident is knowing. It is powerful to know that with God, no matter what, you will not fail. A confident person has poise, a certain attitude about themselves that let those around them know the love and caring they possess.

[59] https://www.blueletterbible.org/kjv/phl/1/6/s_1104006

I am confident of your love for me when I see what you have done for me over the years. You have kept me from danger unseen. You have opened doors for me when I did not see a way. You have allowed doors to stay closed when you knew it would not be to my benefit. You have allowed me to be a blessing by providing me with an abundance of your spirit.

I am content with what you have given me stewardship over, I am confident that you will give me power to handling any circumstance or situation that shows up during my watch. Thank you, Jesus!

Days 98-99-100-101: Power in the name of Jesus

That at the name of Jesus every knee should bow, of things in heaven, and things in earth, and things under the earth;
-Philippians 2:10 (KJV)[60]

What's his name? Jesus! Call him in the morning, noon day, and late in the evening. He said he will answer. When you call him, and is sincere about it, prepare yourself to receive the answer. He may not answer you in the way you "Think" he ought to, but He will answer.

Jesus!

Sometimes you do not have the time to get into the religious posture or use the quiet referential spiritual tone in

---

[60] https://www.blueletterbible.org/kjv/phl/2/10/s_1105010

prayer. Sometimes all you have time to say or can think of to say is JESUS!

We travel a lot. We had purchased tickets headed for Anaheim California from Roxboro North Carolina with a stopover at the O'Hare International airport in Chicago. About the time the O'Hare airport came into view, I noticed that we circled over several times. While circling, we could hear a mechanical whining of gears.

About the fourth time around the airport, the pilot made an announcement that the landing gear was not properly opening and that we were circling to burn fuel for an emergency landing.

As the flight attendants prepped the passengers, a young child made the announcement that, we are going to crash and die! I thought, not with me on here! I am a child of God! It dawned on me that this was real and if I was going to speak anything, it better be positive. So I began chanting Jesus! Jesus! Jesus! Jesus!

Glory to God, the landing gear came down and we landed safely! Was it because of the name of Jesus?

Once we call on Jesus, our next action is to be obedient. Jesus said why call me if you are not going to do what I tell you to do. Sometimes his answer is wait. Will you? Or will you be like so many in the Bible that tried to help God out by being impatience.

Today, if there are challenges coming my way, or when I am down and out and feel like all hope is gone, it is good to have relatives, friends, and extended family to call on. But suppose I am not near a phone, my cell is dead, or I am in a drop zone; no Wi-Fi; no internet connection... Jesus! Oh, how I love the name Jesus! I will give you all the honor and glory. There is no other name to call on that can be a help to all my needs.

Days 102-103-104-105: Power to be Obedient

Woe unto them! For they have gone in the way of Cain, and ran greedily after the error of Balaam for reward, and perished in the gainsaying of Core
- Jude 1:11 (KJV)[61]

Who was Core? In Numbers 16, a "***disobedient***" Levite by the name of Korah (different spelling, same person) drew a following behind him and rebelled against Moses. Korah had decided that he and his crew were just as "holy" as Moses and were demanding some share of the leadership and control. To give a little more clarity, during that time, Moses and Aaron were the spokespersons for the Lord, with authority and direct instructions from God.

What is gainsaying? Some theologians speak of gainsaying to mean against the Word. Looking at the thesaurus, gainsaying, opposing, naysaying, contradicting, arguing, refuting, was Korah's denial of the authority of Moses as God's chosen spokesman. In addition, Korah wanted to intrude into the priest's office.

Although Israel had just come through several major miracles those rebelling was in the middle of trying to choose a captain to go back into Egypt. Korah led this opposition to stop God's direction through Moses.

Today, that would be equivalent to insisting that science (or philosophy or theology) is just as holy as the text of Scripture. God's method of testing this controversy was simple: Each

---

[61] https://www.blueletterbible.org/kjv/

leader was to prepare his own censer and incense (equivalent to his interpretation of God's Word) and see how God responded to him.[62]

Korah, three other rebel leaders and their families were supernaturally killed when the earth opened and swallowed them alive. Two hundred fifty of their followers were also supernaturally killed by fire at the same time.[63] After this happened, there were other Israelites that murmured complained, and blamed God for what had happened to Korah and his crew. Evidently, they had not learned from what had happened. God told Moses to move away from this group of people. God then punished 14,700 men with a plague for objecting to his destruction of Korah, his cohorts, families, and followers.

All disobedience, defiance, noncompliance, insubordination, is sin. God does not tolerate rejection of His message. Today help me to hear and obey your and those you have sent, leadership! Thank you, Jesus, for the power to be obedient.

Days 106-107-108-109: Power to Appreciate the People of God

***Blessed** be he that cometh in the name of the LORD: we have blessed you out of the house of the LORD - Psalm 118:26 (KJV)[64]*

This verse was fulfilled in a preliminary way when Jesus rode into Jerusalem on a small donkey just one week before His resurrection, thereby acknowledging that He was fulfilling

---

[62] http://www.icr.org/article/korahs-dispute/

[63] https://www.blueletterbible.org/kjv/num/16/1/s_133001

[64] https://www.blueletterbible.org/kjv/

Zechariah's prophecy (Zechariah 9:9). As He rode into the city, many took branches of palm trees, and went to meet him, and said, "Hosanna: Blessed is the King of Israel that cometh in the name of the Lord" (John 12:13). Many Christians even today still commemorate that occasion on what they call Palm Sunday, one week before Easter.

But most of the people—now as well as then—doubted and soon rejected him altogether, crying out for him to be put to death. He knew, of course, that this is what would happen. The prophecy applied especially to the nation, but the principle certainly applies also to individuals. Today when anyone sees in his mind's eye the Lord Jesus coming, if he will welcome him gladly rather than turn him away, then Christ will indeed come into his heart, "having salvation" and bringing "joy unspeakable and full of glory" (1 Peter 1:8), and he can say with deep thanks: "Blessed be he that cometh in the name of the LORD."

Days 110-111-112-113: Power to Serve

The disciple is not above his master,
nor the servant above his lord.
- Matthew 10:24 (KJV)[65]

Thank you, Lord, for being my Lord and Savior. From the Holy Scriptures, we are to be disciples and servants of Jesus. To do this we must have a humble-teachable spirit. The word "master" is the same as "teacher." The Lord Jesus, therefore, is our teacher, and He teaches us through His Word—the Holy Scriptures. It is our function to learn His teachings and, of course, to believe them. No Christian (one under the authority

---

[65] https://www.blueletterbible.org/kjv/

of Christ) has the right to reject or even to question one of the teachings of His Word.

Serve God to Get Stuff?

As we were preparing for church and discussing the Sunday school lesson this morning, my grandson, answered the question of, why do we serve God? With to get stuff. We all laughed and continue to discuss the fact that we all are servants and that we serve in different capacities.

But you know, it dawned on me that many Christians feel the same way about serving God. He is the Santa of our wish list. If we are nice enough, (attend Wednesday night bible study, Sunday service, and usher every 2nd Sunday) we will receive the things on our list.

God wants to bless us, but he wants more to have a relationship with us. Seek God first and he will add the "stuff".

The lord-servant relationship goes even further. The word for "servant" is actually "bond slave." The "lord" of a slave was his owner; the word itself means "supreme ruler" and is the title commonly assigned to God himself in the New Testament. Thus, if a disciple is to believe the word of his master without question, the servant is to obey the word of his lord without hesitation.

But the world scoffs at the teachings of God's Word and will try to persecute those who seek to follow them. The unbelieving world—even the religious world—responded to the teachings of Jesus by ridiculing him, then torturing him, and finally hanging him on a tree to die.

Yet we are to go to the same world with the same teachings. Jesus prayed for us, "Remember the word that I said unto you, the servant is not greater than his lord. If they have persecuted me, they will also persecute you; if they have kept my saying, they will keep yours also"[66]. Lord, help me to keep my focus on you when the world come after me.

Days 114-115-116-117: Power to Stay Focused

Remember the former things of old, for I am God and there is none else. I am God and there is none like me.
- Isaiah 46:9: (KJV)[67]

There are so many distractions in my life today. I go to check my email and get side tracked by a pop-up ad. Or I am working diligently and the phone rings. It is a telemarketer wanting to sell me a home security device.

Lord help me to keep you in my focus today. You are everything to me. I will not look back at past failures. If I do, give me the strength and power to praise you for bringing me out.

Help me to put you first but stay focused on the tasks at hand. Whether it be working on the job, completing class assignments, shopping for my family, or making routine decisions, give me wisdom to make the right decision.

It's Her Birthday, Help me Lord!

My daughter died November 15, 2013, leaving us to raise her two children, 10 and 8 years old at that time. It has been over five years now. The grandchildren are now 15 and is 13.

[66] https://www.blueletterbible.org/kjv/jhn/15/20/s_1012020
[67] https://www.blueletterbible.org/kjv/

I am struggling not to be distracted and get back on track with the joy of the Lord and living this life. My daughter's birthday was January 31, which was yesterday. I answered no phones, did no writing, and stayed in the house, talking to the Lord.

Thank God for an understanding spouse. He is retired and works two jobs part-time; school bus driver and truck driver for a local government industry for the disabled. He allowed me to have alone "me and God" time. He made his school pickup for the company and then took our middle school child to the high school basketball game with him. They returned from the game around 9:15 and found me in perfect peace! My regular jovial self!

Jesus, you promised to keep me in perfect peace if I keep my mind on you. Although there are many distractions and challenges, help me to keep my focus on you and the current situation. Thank you for doing just that!

Days 118-119-120-121: Power of Communion

The grace of the Lord Jesus Christ, and the love of God, and the communion of the Holy Ghost, be with you all. Amen
- II Corinthians 13:14 (KJV)[68]

Communion according to several sources is the exchange or sharing of intimate thoughts and feelings especially on a spiritual level. It is also a service of Christian worship at which

---

[68] https://www.blueletterbible.org/kjv/

bread and wine are consecrated and shared in remembrance of celebrating the forgiveness found in Jesus Christ.

The power of communion is more than a memorial. Communion is a powerfully symbolic ceremony that:

- molds our thinking
- Brings to life deeply spiritual truths in very concrete ways.
- Shapes our identity as a people of God
- Provides assurance that we have been redeemed by the blood of the Lamb.

Communion of the Holy Ghost gives us the power to elevate our relationships with one another with glad and sincere hearts. "The grace of the Lord Jesus Christ, and the love of God, and the communion of the Holy Ghost, be with you all. Amen."

Days 122-123-124: Power to Love

And to know the love of Christ, which passes knowledge, that ye might be filled with all the fullness of God -Ephesians 3:19 (KJV)[69]

We say we love everything from our favorite TV show, to our pets to our favorite food—a plate of baked spaghetti.— yum, yum Love can take many forms. There is love we feel for our family, a child and a friend, as well as the love we feel for our pets. There is the in love feeling we feel towards a sweetheart. Do you love yourself? Are we supposed to?

---

[69] https://www.blueletterbible.org/kjv/

Many people think that loving yourself is prideful or vanity. Loving yourself at its core is self-acceptance of who you are just as you are. Loving the good and not-so-good parts of yourself. It's about self-respect and self-empowerment. It's about self-care and looking after yourself and having compassion for yourself when you are going through a hard time. Is this wrong? NO!

In the Old Testament, Leviticus, 19[70] tells us to love the stranger as we love ourselves. In the New Testament, Ephesians 5[71] tells husbands to love their wives as they love themselves. And in the entire book of John, we are told to love one another as God loved us. God is love and he wants us to love him, ourselves, and others.

The depth of his sacrificial love for us surpasses knowledge. His love for us overpowers any love we have for him or for one another. God is love. Love is the fundamental essence of His nature and character.[1] God is perfect in love. God's love is manifested by His absolutely pure desire to care for, share and give to his sons and daughters.

Romans 8 list many aspects of the loving work he has done and is still doing for us. We are fully covered by His love. It asks, "Who shall separate us from the love of Christ?" followed by a carefully worded list of the things that cannot sever our place in His favor, our secure position in Christ.

The section closes with the affirmation "I am persuaded, that neither death, nor life, nor angels, nor principalities, nor powers, nor things present, nor things to come, Nor height, nor depth, nor any other creature, shall be able to separate us from the love of God, which is in Christ Jesus our Lord" "The grace of the Lord Jesus Christ, and the love of God,

[70] https://www.blueletterbible.org/kjv/lev/19/34/s_109034
[71] https://www.blueletterbible.org/kjv/eph/5/33/s_1102033

and the communion of the Holy Ghost, be with you all. Amen"[72]

Days 125-126-127-128: Power Of Favor

For I know the thoughts that I think toward you, said the LORD, thoughts of peace and not of evil, to give you an expected end.
-Jeremiah 29:11 (KJV)[73]

Thank you, Lord for thinking positive thoughts about me. The issue is sometimes I don't think good thoughts about myself. The favor of God is upon my life. This means that God has chosen me to be a recipient of his grace. I did not do anything to earn it. He has blessed me physically, intellectually, financially, emotionally, or socially. He has intentions that these blessings bestowed on me be used to help someone else.

Sometimes people see the favor of God as receiving material thing at someone else's expense. That is why some people say, "Favor isn't fair". Grace is the favor of God on our lives. We must be prepared to receive favor by faith.

Lord, I know there is nothing that I can hide from you. My thoughts, mind, body and soul. You know it all. God, when you tell me that you want me to have a more abundantly life, I know that you give good things, blessings, and not bad.

If it is good, it is God If it is bad, it is the devil. Lord, thank you for giving me eternal life AND the ability to live holy and in peace in this present world.

---

[72] https://www.blueletterbible.org/kjv/rom/8/1/s_1054001
[73] https://www.blueletterbible.org/kjv/

Days 129-130-131-132: Power of Hope

*But it is written, Eye hath not seen, nor ear heard,
neither have entered the heart of man, the things
which God hath prepared for them that love him.
I Corinthians 2:9 (KJV)*[74]

What is hope? If you had to explain it to someone, could you? To truly answer this, you will need to have a personal experience with God. To do that, you must search the scriptures, trust them that they are true, and seek God for understanding. Hope has many like words: expectation, confidence, anticipation, optimism and courage just to name a few.

I love Jesus always and he blesses me day by day. Lord, increase my faith. I am a visual person, but I know faith is the substance of things hoped for the evidence of things not seen. Lord, only you have numbered the hairs on my head. Lord, you know the number of my days.

Help me to make this and every day one of thanksgiving and praise to you. Lord, when I think I have seen it all, you amaze me again and again.

I expect and have confidence that you will do what you said you will do. Thank you for the courage to wait during the anticipation.

Days 133-134-135-136: Power to Remember

*Remember the former things of old: For I am God, and
there is none else; I am God, and there is none like me.
- Isaiah 46: 9 (KJV)*[75]

---

[74] https://www.blueletterbible.org/kjv/

[75] https://www.blueletterbible.org/kjv/

Thank you, God, for what you have done, is doing and is going to do! Thank you for your display of love time and time again in the scriptures to those that love you and keep your commandments. Time after time the Word of God has been challenged and always prove to be true.

As I was meditating on your words, I ran across the Holy Communion. You said to eat the bread, representing your body, and drink the wine, representing your blood, in remembrance of you.[76] What really was mind blowing is when you said for this reason there are many are sick and weakly among you because of not remembering what you had done for us.

All the prophecies that have come true stands as proof to the validity of the Bible. Science has pulled out every new technological discovery only to help prove that the Bible is true. Thank you, Jesus!

Days 137-138-139-140: Power to Receive God's Strength

For as the heaven is high above the earth, so great is his mercy toward them that fear him.
- Psalm 103:11 (KJV)[77]

God has not given us the spirit of fear, but of power, and of love and of a sound mind. Sounds conflicting, doesn't it? He does not want us to be afraid of him such as shaking in our shoes, scared. This fear is not speaking of dread, anxiety, or distress. This fear is a reverence of God. This is a showing or respect, awe, admiration, or worship.

---

[76] https://www.blueletterbible.org/kjv/1co/11/30/s_1073030
[77] https://www.blueletterbible.org/kjv/

A few older people hold traditions of reverence of the Lord, but the majority of mankind is trying to put you out of everything they do. They think they are moving and doing by their own strength. Don't pray in schools, it offends me. Don't pray at public events, it offends me. Many that are serving the devil will boldly state that you must accept me for who I am and my lifestyle. While they on the other hand show no respect or care for the people of God.

Stand firm on God's word and draw from His strength. Rejoice and be glad that God has given you another day to make things right.

Thank you for your grace and mercy, it endures forever. The joy of the Lord is truly my strength!

Days 141-142-143-144: Power over Deception

For God hath not given us the spirit of fear; but of power, and of love, and of a sound mind.
- II Timothy 1:7 (KJV)[78]

With all that is going on right now: Rise in prejudice, murder, theft, slander, false accusations, and mayhem, your grace, mercy and precious promises to your people gives us the power over all this deception.

Dishonesty and trickery is the business plan of the world today. But your people can lift their eyes unto he hills where our help comes from.

Your people do not fear the happenings going on in this world. Thank you for keeping us in the ark of safety. We are covered under the blood of Jesus. I rebuke the doubt and fear

---

[78] https://www.blueletterbible.org/kjv/

that the enemy of my soul tries to bring through subtle lies and challenging circumstances.

Thank you, Jesus, for the gift of discernment. For not allowing any harm to come on us unaware. Thank you for the love, the power, and a sound mind.

Days 145-146-147-148: Power to Bear Good Fruit

Not because I desire a gift: but I desire fruit that may abound to your account.
- Philippians 4:17 (KJV) [79]

Genuine traits of godly character are called fruits. "For the fruit of the Spirit is in all goodness and righteousness and truth"[80]. The classic passage, Galatians 5:22[81]: outlines the nine fruit produced by the Holy Spirit in the life of a willing Christian. Those fruit are:

- Love
- Joy
- Peace
- Longsuffering
- Gentleness
- Goodness
- Faith
- Meekness
- Temperance

[79] https://www.blueletterbible.org/kjv/
[80] https://www.blueletterbible.org/kjv/eph/5/9/s_1102009
[81] https://www.blueletterbible.org/kjv/gal/5/22/s_1096022

It is significant that all these attributes constitute one fruit, not nine fruits. The tremendous importance of fruit-bearing in the Christian life is brought out by Christ in His famous sermon on the vine and the branches in John 15:1-16.

When you hear the phrase that the fruit doesn't fall far from the tree, remember to go about doing "good" so people can witness good fruit.

Days 149-150-151-152: Power to Stay Amazed

Open thou mine eyes, that I may behold
wondrous things out of thy law.
-Psalm 119:18 (KJV)[82]

We are amazed as we study the intricate complexity of living creatures—especially human beings and their relationship to God. Children are fascinated by mostly everything. The same for baby Christians. It is exciting to hear how God is moving and working in their lives. They testify to his goodness, grace and mercy. They are excited about their new life.

The people of Jesus' day were astonished at the miracles that he performed and wondered how he could do these healings and miracles being that he was nobody but Joseph's son. They talked among themselves how amazing his teachings were and how the other teachers of the law pale in comparison to him.

What happens to the amazement, when we grow and mature in the word? The cares of this life appear to overshadow the day to day wonders of God. God help us to stay amazed at the sunrise, the blooming flowers, the ability to think and the freedom to praise and worship him. Let us tell of His

---

[82] https://www.blueletterbible.org/kjv/

glory among the nations, His wonderful deeds among all the peoples.[83]

Days 153-154-155-156: Power Overcome Doubt

So then faith comes by hearing and
hearing by the word of God.
- Roman 10:17 (KJV)[84]

Have you ever doubted God? Want to stop doubting him? To stop doubting God, trust must be built. Considering this previous statement, it is hard to trust a stranger, or even an occasional acquaintance. This brings us to your relationship with God. Do you have one?

Christians can overcome doubting God by reading the Bible. Sounds simple, but it is true. When you took the salvation step and the Holy Spirit came to dwell in you, it was the beginning of a lifelong expedition of getting to know God. One thing the Bible makes clear is that God is faithful, trustworthy and good. As we fill our minds with the proofs of God's power and love through experience and history we are better able to overcome doubt.

Consistent Bible reading depending on the Holy Ghost to give us understanding, encourages us, satisfies, and sustains us, and reveals what God is like, what he loves and what he hates. Another way to erase doubt is to pray. Each believing prayer helps to bring us closer in our relationship to him. Prayer is just talking to God.

[83] https://www.blueletterbible.org/kjv/psa/96/3/s_574003
[84] https://www.blueletterbible.org/kjv/rom/10/17/s_1056017

Days 157-158-159-160: Power to be a Holy Temple of God

Know ye not that ye are the temple of God;
and that the Spirit of God dwells in you?
- I Corinthian 3:16 (KJV)[85]

Scripture reveals that God is pleased to dwell among those who have received his atonement and forgiveness. In Moses' time, God dwelled mainly in the tabernacle and later in the temple in Jerusalem. A benefit of the new covenant is that he shows up wherever people gather to worship him. Today we no longer need to make the long journey to a designated city to meet with our holy Creator, because his Spirit dwells within us, his church.

The Holy Spirit dwells in all born again believers. The Spirit joins us together as one temple in whom the fullness of God's presence is enjoyed. It is His will that we should embrace all in holy unity and He in turn form one temple of many. Each person is a temple but when joined to others, each becomes a stone of God's temple—fitting together.

As a believer and a stone in God's temple, to sin against another is to assault His holy dwelling place and bring him grief. Moreover, when we have damaged another brother or sister, we must go to that person, admit our sin, ask for forgiveness, and make restitution if possible. In doing this, we beautify the place where God lives.

---

[85] https://www.blueletterbible.org/kjv/1co/3/16/s_1065016

Days 161-162-163-164: Power to Receive His Love

Beloved, if God so loved us, we ought also to love one another. No man hath seen God at any time. If we love one another, God dwells in us, and his love is perfected in us.
- I John 4:11-12 (KJV)[86]

It is God's will for each of us to be "perfected in love" which means fully developed and mature. God created each of us to become uniquely and fully developed in our ability to love. To receive God's love, one must first love oneself.

Many people strive first to increase in wealth, become physically fit, become popular, advance in their career or just to become plain comfortable. If these things are obtained at the expense of loving your spouse, children, co-workers, neighbors, friends, the poor or even your enemies, you are failing in life.

If you want to be perfected in love, you must develop both the capacity to receive God's love and increase your capacity to give love away to others. Since we cannot give to others what we don't have, first, let us allow God to indwell us with his love, and then continually draw upon God's love.

Days 165-166-167-168: Power to Receive Forgiveness

That Christ may dwell in your hearts by faith; that ye, being rooted and grounded in love).
- Ephesians 3:17 (KJV)[87]

[86] https://www.blueletterbible.org/kjv/1jo/4/12/s_1163012
[87] https://www.blueletterbible.org/kjv/eph/3/17/s_1100017

God's love cannot be earned but was freely extended to us. Even greater than that, his love was given by choice and nature, even when we were still sinners; Christ died for us.

His love for us never fails and never changes: "Jesus Christ the same yesterday, and today, and forever." He was willing to die so that our death penalty would be paid and to adopt us into His family. Even now He rejoices over us. "The LORD thy God amid thee is mighty; he will save, he will rejoice over thee with joy; he will rest in his love, he will joy over thee with singing".

He now oversees us from His place at the right hand of His Father, making intercession for us. Jesus is able also to save them to the utmost that come unto God by him, seeing he ever lives to make intercession for us. Such love is deep indeed. Repent and receive his forgiveness.

Days 169-170-171-172: Power of Protection

This matter is by the decree of the watchers, and the demand by the word of the holy ones: to the intent that the living may know that the most High rules in the kingdom of men, and giveth it to whomsoever he will, and set up over it the basest of men.
- Daniel 4:17 (KJV)[88]

The Bible indicates that "the angels desire to consider" the outworking of the gospel in the hearts of men, and that "unto the principalities and powers in heavenly places might be known by the church the manifold wisdom of God". Children, as well as adult believers, also seem to have guardian angels who "watch" us.

---

[88] https://www.blueletterbible.org/kjv/Daniel 4:7

Protected by the Guardian Angels!

There was this young lady that lived in a small rural town in the south. She had had an altercation with a young man known to be a bully in that place. This guy weighed about 300 pounds and the young lady weighed a good 120 pounds soaking wet. She had literally beat this man "to a pulp" the night before and was told that this man was coming back to kill her and her family. She and her husband had two boys and a girl. This guy had told his brothers and cousins that the person that had so brutally beat him like that was a man; this young lady's brother.

In the meantime, this young lady notified her brother of what was being said and she went to a neighbor to borrow a gun. The neighbor loaned her an unregistered 38 caliber pistol.

During all this drama, a younger sister and her husband came to visit. She did not know what they were walking in to. The guardian angels were dispatched to the little single-wide trailer on the top of the red hill that day. The couple was sitting on the sofa in the living room, when the car topped the hill with shot guns and rifles sticking out of every window. The young lady threw the pistol to her brother who ran into the bedroom to the left of the sofa. She told the children to hide under the bed in the bedroom to the right of the sofa. The car came to a stop in front of the steps.

Six people got out with guns and two went to the left of the trailer, two went to the right of the trailer and two came into the trailer. As they stepped through the door, the young lady's husband spoke, and they shot at him. The bullet missed his head by inches and he ran down the hall. The husband of the visiting sister spoke, and they shot at them both on the sofa. The bullet went between their feet. That's when the brother came out of the bedroom, placed the 38 in the chest of the guy in front, and pulled the trigger. As the guy was falling back out of the door, his shotgun knocked the pistol out of the brother's hand. He ran down the hall and out of the back door! At that time, the sound of the four gunners on each side of the house firing rounds as the young man ran across the field could be heard throughout the neighborhood!

When the second home invader saw that his cousin was shot, he called for the others and they got into the car and left the shot cousin lying on the ground in front of the steps. My sister and I watch him take his last breath at which all his bodily fluids were released.

The guardian angels protected this family that day! None of the occupants were hit by any of the bullets! The young man went to the police station and confessed to killing. The young lady called the police and confessed to killing the guy, also. She ended up convincing the police that she did the actual shooting and that her brother was trying to protect her. In court, the judge looked at all the shell casings, picture of the gun shot holes in the house, and threw the case out and said, "If people came to my house like this, I would have killed him too. Give this young lady her gun back. Case dismissed!"

Guardian angels are a mysterious subject because we cannot see these "watchers," but we at least need to know they are there. In fact, let us praise God that "the angel of the LORD positions themselves around us that fear him, and delivers us". Thank you, Jesus!

We need the power of God's protection because who knows that there may be sinful attitudes and habits lurking in the heart of which one is completely unaware. If you have experienced the failure of your own wisdom, you can develop an appreciation for the power of God's protection.

Days 173-174-175-176: Power to be one with Him

For by one Spirit are we all baptized into one body, whether we be Jews or Gentiles, whether we be bond or free; and have been all made to drink into one Spirit.
- I Corinthian 12:13 (KJV)[89]

Have you been baptized? How were you baptized? In the name of the Father, Son, and the Holy Ghost? In the name of Jesus? In the name of the Father, Son, Holy Ghost, and Jesus' name? Thank you, God, for the baptism in one Spirit, the theme of this passage, teaching us that every one of the "brethren"—those who "speaking by the Spirit of God" have acknowledged Jesus to be their Lord —have been "baptized into one body," the body of Christ himself.

Not in the Same Building, But of the Same Spirit!

My spouse and I joined and had been faithfully attending and supporting this church building for about ten years when God confirmed that our work there had come to an end. We notified leadership. I was called by one of the chief leaders for a meeting.

During the meeting, sadly to say, several accusations were made that really sealed the fact that we were right in leaving. Here is "some" of what I was told:

---

[89] https://www.blueletterbible.org/kjv/

- We at this church building have the truth—going somewhere else will put us out of the will of God.
- The finger nail polish that I was wearing showed that I really did not have God's spirit, therefore, we could not have heard from God about leaving.
- That we were obligated to continue to give tithes and offerings to this church.

I am going to stop right there. If you are in a church building that teach and preach that God only speaks to those in leadership in that building, get out of there! If you are in a church building that attribute God's Spirit to the length of your skirt or the color of your nails, get out of there! If you are in a church building that thinks only they have the truth, get out of there! God is not a respecter of person, nor does he give one person all they need so that they have no need of their fellow man.

That is why true Christians rejoice that the Holy Spirit has placed each of us securely in the body of Christ, united to him and sharing His resurrection life, with all functioning together through "the same God which worked all in all"

When we receive God's Spirit, we are enabled to relate to him in a personal way, like a child relating to his father who deeply loves him. This personal and spiritual bond with God also forges a personal and spiritual bond with other Christians. Becoming one with Him in our mental, emotional and moral lives honor's Jesus and allow others to see how real and good Jesus is and decide to join God's family.

Days 177-178-179-180: Power over Sin and Sinning

In the name of our Lord Jesus Christ, when ye are gathered together, and my spirit, with the power of our Lord Jesus Christ.
- I Corinthian 5:4 (KJV)[90]

The opening words are probably the form used in all public acts of the Church as a body, and "the power of our Lord Jesus" refers to that continual presence which Christ had promised His Church, and power which He had delegated to the Apostles to punish. Do everything in the name of "Jesus"

Paul had been told that someone in the church had committed incest but that the members of the Corinthian church had not reprimanded this person. Paul had warned the Corinthians earlier to not to associate with immoral persons. To explain this statement correctly, one must establish what the sin is that caused Paul to deliver the declaration.

It is the responsibility of the local church in to deal with such a situation. The whole set of circumstances emphasizes how important it is for local churches to implement church-disciplinary actions in dealing with sinning members and to use sound principles in doing so.

Days 181-182-183-184: Power in the Holy Ghost

Then Peter said unto them. Repent, and be baptized every one of you in the name of

---

> *Jesus Christ for the remission of sins, and ye*
> *shall receive the gift of the Holy Ghost.*
> *- Acts 2:38 (KJV)[91]*

Just like the crowd on the day of Pentecost, we must recognize our desolation and our need for a savior. The disciples, in obedience to the command of Jesus, gathered together for prayer, and came together on one accord. They recognized they did not have the resources in themselves to do what they should do. They had to rely on and wait for the power of the Holy Ghost.[92]

The Holy Ghost unites us to Jesus Christ and to His body. The Spirit reveals Christ to us, gives us His life, and makes Christ alive in us. The Spirit takes the experiences of Jesus—His incarnation, ministry, crucifixion, resurrection, and ascension—and brings them into our own experience. Because of the Holy Ghost, the history of Jesus Christ becomes our story and experience

Practically speaking, the Holy Ghost come to live in us to help us to live right love right and go about doing the will of God.

Days 185-186-187-188: Power in Obedience

> *And this is his commandment that we should*
> *believe on the name of his Son Jesus Christ, and*
> *love one another, as he gave us commandment.*
> *- I John 3:23 (KJV)[93]*

---

[91] https://www.blueletterbible.org/kjv/

[92] http://calvaryglenwood.org/the-importance-of-unity/

[93] https://www.blueletterbible.org/kjv/

And this is his commandment…, Having mentioned the keeping of the commandments of God, the apostle proceeds to show what they are; that they are faith in Christ, and love to one another; which two are reduced to one, because they are inseparable; where the one is, the other is; faith works by love.

We can believe a document, or a statement, or a person; but how can we believe a name? By believing those truths which the name implies: in the present case by believing that Jesus is the Savior, is the Messiah, is the Son of God. To produce this belief and its consequence, eternal life, is the purpose of St. John's Gospel; it is also the will of God, and the command of Jesus.

This belief will inevitably produce as its fruit that we "love one another, even as Christ gave us commandment".

Thank you for the power to be obedient to the your divine commands.—to love you with all my heart,

Days 189-190-191-192: Power in the Name of Jesus

Then Peter said, Silver and gold have I none,
but such as I have give I thee. In the name of
Jesus Christ of Nazareth rise up and walk.
- Act 3:6 (KJV)[94]

Leaders of congregations should be preaching the Gospel of Jesus Christ and giving through service to God's people. However, GREED has crept into the Church and deception has invaded God's people, which is the Church, not four walls or a puppet on stage. It is sickening what is happening today but as long as the people allow, it will continue. Just

---

[94] https://www.blueletterbible.org/kjv/

stay dumb and be sure to pay your tithes and offerings and by the way you must follow all the law and not just one or two verses.

Peter explained the miracle of the lame man walking by saying, "The faith which is by Jesus has given this man strong bones and the ability to walk." Even the faith which they spoke was from Jesus. Jude says, "Earnestly contend for the faith which was once for all entrusted to the Saints."

Jesus said those who believe in him would also do the works that He did. 1 Cor. 12:9 says faith is a spiritual gift and Eph.6:11 and 16 tell us to take it and put it on. Beyond our human faith, the faith of Jesus is entrusted to us to use for His glory. Let's press for the prize of the high calling of God in Christ Jesus. (Phil. 3:14)

Days 193-194-195-196: Power to be Bold

Be it known unto you all, and to all the people of Israel, that by the name of Jesus Christ of Nazareth, whom ye crucified whom God raised from the dead, even by him doth this man stand here before you whole.
- Act 4:10 (KJV)[95]

The boldness of the Peter's declaration was startling. He does not shrink now from confessing the Nazarene as the Messiah. He presses home the fact that, though Pilate had given the formal sentence, it was they who had crucified their King. He proclaims that He has been raised from the dead and is still as a Power working to heal as when on earth.

Peter being filled with the Holy Ghost, would have all to understand, that the miracle had been wrought by the

---

[95] https://www.blueletterbible.org/kjv/

name, or power, of Jesus of Nazareth, the Messiah, whom they had crucified; and this confirmed their testimony to his resurrection from the dead, which proved him to be the Messiah. These rulers must either be saved by that Jesus whom they had crucified, or they must perish forever. The name of Jesus is given to men of every age and nation, as that whereby alone believers are saved from the wrath to come.

But when covetousness, pride, or any corrupt passion, rules within, men shut their eyes, and close their hearts, in enmity against the light; considering all as ignorant and unlearned, who desire to know nothing in comparison with Christ crucified.

The followers of Christ behave in such a way so that all who come into contact with them will say what they said of the apostles, "These people know and have been with Jesus." That makes them holy, heavenly, spiritual, and cheerful, and raises them above this world.

Days 197-198-199-200 Power to Preach

But when they believed Philip preaching the things concerning the kingdom of God and the name of Jesus Christ, they were baptized, both men and women.
- Act 8:12 (KJV)[96]

What is preaching? Sometimes to get an understanding of a principle or thought, you need to understand the meaning words and how they are used. According to the thesaurus, preaching has many synonyms, from the word proselytization to speaking. To speak, talk or expound are the words I prefer to identify preach.

---

[96] https://www.blueletterbible.org/kjv/

The Great Commission instructed the apostles to preach the gospel to every creature of every nation of the world. In order for this to happen, they had to leave Jerusalem and be scattered. Among those who were scattered abroad was Philip the evangelist, one of the seven chosen in Acts 6 to serve in administering the benevolent needs of the widows.

Those chosen for that work were "of honest report, full of the Holy Ghost and wisdom" (Acts 6:3). This God-fearing, honorable man went to Samaria and preached the gospel to the Samaritans. Here is the record per Luke.

What did Philip preach?

1. Christ to the Samaritans. The Samaritan people accepted the Pentateuch as a revelation of God and, therefore, had an expectation of the coming of the Messiah.
2. The things concerning the kingdom of God. The newer translations say that Philip preached the good news of the kingdom of God.
3. The name of Jesus. By preaching the name of Jesus, Philip identified the promised Messiah with the man Jesus of Nazareth. No doubt, he told the Samaritans of his death, burial, and resurrection, explaining that he shed his blood on Calvary for the sins of man. After being raised from the dead, he ascended into heaven to be seated at the right hand of God.

Philip cast out demons and healed those who were palsied or lame. The Lord promised that miracles would accompany the preaching of the gospel and explained that their purpose was to confirm the message which was preached.

Days 201-202-203-204: Power in the Name

And this did she many days. But Paul, being grieved, turned and said to the spirit. I command thee in the name of Jesus Christ to come out of her. And he came out the same hour.
- Act 16:18 (KJV)[97]

We have that Power! Do you exercise it? Do you have enough holy boldness to speak to the issues and challenges in your life in the Name of Jesus?

When your head is aching, what do you do? When your children are cutting up in public, what do you do? When you get out of bed in the morning and your joints are aching, what do you do? When you take medication, what do you do?

Talk to your body for physical deliverance. Say, joints stop aching in Jesus name. By His stripes, I am healed. Speak to your finances. I am the lender and not the borrower, in Jesus' name. Speak to your children. Tell them what they will do in Jesus name. Speak to any issue or circumstance you are facing.

Decide today to speak what God word says in the Name of Jesus!

Days 205-206-207-208 Power to be Sanctified

Unto the church of God which is at Corinth, to them that are sanctified in Christ Jesus, called to be saints, with all that in every place call upon the name of Jesus Christ our Lord, both theirs and ours.
- I Corinthians 1:2 (KJV)[98]

---

[97] https://www.blueletterbible.org/kjv/
[98] https://www.blueletterbible.org/kjv/

Sanctification is the progress toward holiness. That's spiritual growth. That's becoming increasingly separated from sin and separated unto Jesus Christ. Sanctification begins at our salvation and it ends or culminates at our glorification. We are justified, declared righteous at our salvation. We are glorified, made fully righteous when we see the Lord face to face. In the meantime, we are being progressively sanctified. That is, we are progressively being separated from sin unto Christ.

The Jews had thoughts about this word "sanctify" which brought it more helpfully within the sphere of their actual life and labor. To them to sanctify a thing was to take it away - to separate it from common uses, and devote it wholly, consecrate it, to Divine and holy uses. A person or a thing was sanctified when it was given over wholly to God and God's service

For their sakes, O Father, I am sanctifying myself.'" And there we learn that most blessed lesson that "sanctity is power" - power to honor the Divine Name, power to redeem and uplift our fellow-men.

Days 209-210-211-212: Power in Bowing

That at the name of Jesus every knee should bow, of thing in heaven, and things in earth, and things under the earth - Philippians 2:10 (KJV)[99]

Bowing, also called genuflection, is much more than Anglican aerobics or even a "churchy" ritual. Bowing or genuflection is also not groveling under the eyes of some tyrannical God who expects fear or some unhealthy sense of self-worthlessness from us. Bowing or genuflecting is an act

---

[99] https://www.blueletterbible.org/kjv/

of humility not humiliation. Humility comes from the Latin word humus meaning earth or ground. If we join our hearts with our bodies when bowing or genuflecting it may help us "to come down to earth".

Bowing may remind us to be "grounded" in our own reality, a reality that is need of God's grace and healing. Bowing may help us remember that we are not the center of the universe – God is. A bow or genuflection may be a simple and helpful reminder that God and our neighbor come first.

When we bow or genuflect, we acknowledge the Master into whose House we have come. A Master who himself was humble of heart, and who bowed down to the floor to wash the feet of his friends and who ate and drank with outcasts and sinners – a Master who chose to be a servant and who desires us to follow his example.

Days 213-214-215: Power to be Holy

***Having therefore, brethren, boldness to enter
into the holiest by the blood of Jesus.
- Hebrew 10:19 (KJV)[100]***

The agreement of infinite holiness with pardoning mercy, was not clearly understood till the human nature of Christ, the Son of God, was wounded, bruised, and shed his blood for our sins. Our way to heaven is by a crucified Savior; his death is to us the way of life, and to those who believe this, he will be precious.

We must draw near to God; it would be contempt of Christ, still to keep at a distance. Our bodies are to be washed with pure water, alluding to the cleansings directed under

---

[100] https://www.blueletterbible.org/kjv/

the law: thus, the use of water in baptism, was to remind Christians that our conduct should be pure and holy.

While we derive comfort and grace from our reconciled Father to our own souls, we would adorn the doctrine of God our Savior in all things. Believers are to consider how we can be of service to each other, especially stirring up each other to the more vigorous and abundant exercise of love, and the practice of good works. The communion of saints is a great help and privilege, and a means of steadfastness and perseverance

Days 216-217-218-219: Power to Speak No Evil

But Jesus said, forbid him not: for there
is no man which shall do a miracle in my
name that can lightly speak evil of me.
- Mark 9:39 (KJV)[101]

Too often have churches and their teachers not acted when men were doing the work of Christ, combating evil, relieving wants, in irregular ways, or with imperfect faith. In all such cases, we need to remember the words "Forbid him not . . . he that is not against us is on our side."

The words "lightly or quickly" are wide-reaching in their range. The true Disciples of Christ are to hinder no one who is doing the work Jesus told them to do. The very fact that they do it will bring with it reverence and sympathy. They will not "quickly" be found among those who speak evil of the Son of Man.

Moses' sister, Miriam, was struck with leprosy for bad mouthing Moses. God does not take lightly evil speaking about his children. Since we all belong to God, it would be wise for us not to speak evil of no man.

---

[101] https://www.blueletterbible.org/kjv/

Lord, help me to watch what I say concerning you and your children.

Days 220-221-222-223: Power to Bear Witness

> *Jesus answered them, I told you, and ye*
> *believed not, the works that I do in my*
> *Father's name, they bear witness of me.*
> *- John 10:25 (KJV)[102]*

When Jesus said, I told you before what I tell you now again, that the works which I do, bear testimony to me. I have told you that I am the light of the world: The Son of God: the good shepherd: that I am come to save - to give life - to give liberty - to redeem you: that, in order to this, I must die, and rise again; and that I am absolute master of my life, and of my death.

Those that were always around him and followed had not noticed. Jesus was saying, "Have you not noticed my omniscience, in searching and discovering the very secrets of your hearts? Have you not seen my omnipotence in the miracles which I have wrought? Have not all these been sufficient to convince you? - and yet ye will not believe!" - See the works which bore testimony to him, as the Messiah in Matthew 11:5 and listed below:

The blind receive sight

The lame walk

Those who have leprosy are cleansed

The deaf hear

The dead are raised, and

The good news is proclaimed to the poor

Lord, help me to see you at work in my life each day.* * *

[102] https://www.blueletterbible.org/kjv/

Days 224-225-226-227: Power to Believe

But these are written, that ye might believe that Jesus is the Christ, the Son of God, and that believing ye might have life through his name.
- John 20:31 (KJV)[103]

Do you believe the Bible? It is amazing how quickly the average internet surfer believes Facebook posts, Twitter feeds, and other social media information—even what is broadcasted on the evening news. In looking at today's scripture text, there were other signs and proofs of our Lord's resurrection, but these were committed to writing, that all might believe that Jesus was the promised Messiah, the Savior of sinners, and the Son of God; that, by this faith, they might obtain eternal life, by his mercy, truth, and power.

If we can believe that Jesus came through the Virgin Mary; Lived and experienced in a human body; took on our infirmities and went to the cross in our place; rose on the third day and is seated on the right hand of God, we will have eternal life!

Abundant blessings are in store for all of us that believe that Jesus is the Christ. From our faith in the truth of the word of God, we will have life through His name!

Days 228-229-230-231: Power to Heal

By stretching forth thine hand to heal; and that signs and wonders may be done by the name of thy holy child Jesus.
- Acts 4:30 (KJV)[104]

---

[103] https://www.blueletterbible.org/kjv/
[104] https://www.blueletterbible.org/kjv/

Why would anyone not want to be healed? One of the most controversial subjects among the Christian community is the topic of healing. Even though scripture clearly speaks to healing because of the stripes Jesus endured before going to the cross, some religious groups have a problem with receiving healing.

Christians in the early church, before Jesus' stripes, experienced miracles of healing as well. Look at Jesus' healing miracles. The Bible shows us that he healed:

- By the Word
- By the faith of the sick
- To release service
- To restore life
- To deliver from demons
- Through the faith of others besides the sick
- Through the faith of the desperate and persistent
- To reveal God and God's heart
- His enemies

Therefore, we as His body must release His healing power to our generation too! Lord, thank you for the power to heal!

Days 232-233-234-235: Power to be Thankful

Giving thanks always for all things unto God and the Father in the name of our Lord Jesus Christ.
- Ephesians 5:20 (KJV)[105]

Are you thankful? Thankfulness is the key that turns your situation around because it changes you, your outlook,

---

[105] https://www.blueletterbible.org/kjv/

and your attitude. Thankfulness is how we move into higher realms of faith for ourselves and every aspect of our lives. Giving thanks during difficulty bring pleasure to God's heart and breakthrough begins.

Being thankful in all things is not always easy, but it is a "must do" to see God's will accomplished in our lives. There is power in a thankful heart. Thanksgiving brings contentment. An attitude of thanksgiving accepts and embraces God's will. Practice thankfulness by praising God for everything in your life, don't allow yourself to complain about anything, and stop comparing yourself with others.

Discontent, otherwise complaining, dries up the soul. Begin to thank God for all the blessings he has given instead of dwelling on the negative. To learn to be people of praise and thanksgiving to God all the days of our lives would be a great accomplishment. There is greatness and happiness in thanks giving.[106]

Days 236-237-238-239: Power to Assemble with Others

In the name of our Lord Jesus Christ, when ye are gathered together, and my spirit, with the power of our Lord Jesus Christ - I Corinthians 5:4 (KJV)[107]

Why don't you want to get together with fellow Christians? Christians are to help each other hang on to the end by encouraging each other not to become complacent or lazy.

---

[106] https://www.crosswalk.com/faith/prayer/the-power-of-a-thankful-heart.html

[107] https://www.blueletterbible.org/kjv/

To do this, we must assemble ourselves together. It is hard to encourage or receive encouragement when not with other Christians. Do you know any Christian who plans to sit at home reading and learning about God?

A group of spirit filled believers is a powerful force to be reckon with when we gather together, pray, exhorting one another, and encouraging one another.

Not assembling with other Christians is one of the dangerous symptoms of backsliding. It is your personal duty to be faithful, care for others, and to exhort one another. The assembling of ourselves has unspeakable value:

- Strengthening of the faith, hope and love
- For the full development of a holy life
- For the helping and comforting of all who are feeble
- For the cultivation of the fellowship of the Spirit and the Word * * *

Days 240-241-242-243: Power to be One

Now I beseech you brethren by the name of our Lord Jesus Christ, that ye all speak the same thing, and that there be no divisions among you, but that ye be perfectly joined together in the same mind and the same judgment.
- I Corinthian 1:10 (KJV)[108]

When Paul says, you should all speak the same thing it means we should all speak the word of God: the same message Paul spoke. He is referring to a simplicity of faith. The more complex a person's spiritual thinking becomes the less likely there can be unity in this regard.

---

[108] https://www.blueletterbible.org/kjv/

Deeply "religious" people can get so offended and want to argue or debate over little of nothing. Most disagreements among the congregation are over things that are menial. Things such as what color curtains to put to the windows or what dish to bring to the dinner, are issues brought on by the people themselves. Many of these issues arise from traditions. To really experience the power of unity, search the scriptures, pray about everything, and rely less on opinions. Appeal to Scripture to examine the interpreters of Scripture. That's if you desire unity.

Lord, help us to be one in mind and sound doctrine.

Days 244-245-246-247: Power to Have Faith

Now faith is the substance of things hope
for, the evidence of things not seen
-Hebrews 11:1 (KJV)[109]

What does it mean to have faith? There are many definitions of which, I adhere to the one that says faith is belief and trust in and loyalty to God.

We were chosen by Christ himself. Like the disciples, we were first witnesses, then preachers, of the resurrection of Christ, and so of the entire gospel-dispensation, —our gifts are excellent and extraordinary.

Like the apostles, we have a power of working miracles, not at all times, but when Christ pleased. We are led into all truth, endowed with the spirit of prophecy, and have an extent of power and jurisdiction beyond all others.

Hence learn, a believer may lawfully acknowledge, and sometimes is bound to assert, the gifts and graces of God to

---

[109] https://www.blueletterbible.org/kjv/heb/11/1/s_1144001

him. If we pretend to have his spirit and anointing and we do not is hypocrisy; to deny that we have these things when we do is ingratitude.

It concerns all, but especially ministers, to consider well their warrant and call from God to their work. This will justify them to others, and give them inward support and comfort under all dangers and discouragements.

Days 248-249-250-251: Power to be Cleanse from All Sin

But if we walk in the light, as he is in the light, we have fellowship one with another, and the blood of Jesus Christ his Son cleanses us from all sin.
- I John 1:7 (KJV)[110]

Ever whished the things Jesus did for people we read about tin the bible was our experience? Through faith in Jesus Christ, they were able to accomplish the most astonishing achievements, or were rescued from sad plights or gained tremendous new power over difficulties. That power can be yours. Hebrews states, "Jesus Christ is the same yesterday, today, and forever."

Jesus Christ never changes and is an invariable factor in a variable world. He is just the same now as when He walked the shores of Galilee. He has the same kindness, the same power to heal and change men's lives. He is the same restorer of courage the same transformer of people souls.

Anything that He ever did for anyone throughout all

---

[110] https://www.blueletterbible.org/kjv/

history, He can do for you. It all depends upon how completely you surrender yourself to him and how sincerely you believe.

Lord help me to believe and receive.

Days 252-253-254-255: Power to Have Life Abundantly

Then Jesus said unto them, Verily, verily, I say unto you. Except ye eat the flesh of the Son of man, and drink his blood, ye have no life in you.
- John 6:53 (KJV)[111]

Have you ever stopped to think that in the Holy Ghost that is within you, you have the power of God that created the universe? If you come to the understanding of this, you would no longer be the victim of depression, rage, drug addiction, and all those demonic spirits that come to kill, steal, and destroy. Learn to believe and cast out doubt. This is done by practice of affirmation. Affirm faith, think positively, and visualize achievement.

The inner power is simply the God given ability to believe. To the extent to which you develop this faculty, you will master the defeats in your live. The great issue is to learn to believe. Mark 9:23 says it like this: "Jesus said to him, "If you can believe all things are possible to him who believes."

Mark affirms that when you learn to believe, the area of the impossible is vastly reduced and the area of the possible is greatly increased. If you set this scripture firmly at the center of your thought patterns, you will never again be a victim

---

[111] https://www.blueletterbible.org/kjv/

of low spirits. Lord Help me to believe! Thank you for my abundant Life!

Days 256-257-258-259: Power to Get Close to God

*But now is Christ Jesus ye who sometimes were
far off are made nigh by the blood of Christ.
- Ephesians 2:13 (KJV)*[112]

Joy has healing value, but gloom is sickening. Therefore, Jesus so emphatically tells us to rejoice. Learn to live joyfully. Take a hopeful and optimistic attitude. Develop that relationship with God through the blood of the Lamb.

You can think happy thoughts, say positive, encouraging things, and bring joy into the lives of people you meet. The more you do this the more surely you will draw near to God and keep your own spirit high. When you apply the blood, it:

- Provides forgiveness of your sins
- Gives your life meaning
- Brings you close to God
- Cleanses your conscience
- Gives you boldness to approach God
- Sanctifies you
- Cleanses you
- Heals you
- Enables you to overcome the devil and his works

---

[112] https://www.blueletterbible.org/kjv/

Lord, thank you for allowing me the opportunity to get closer to you.

Days 260-261-262-263: Power to Forgive

And to Jesus the mediator of the new covenant, and to the blood of sprinkling, that speaketh better things than that of Abel - Hebrew 12:24 (KJV)[113]

The word of Jesus Christ, when recorded in consciousness and held there, can make you clean of all guilt. How you ask? The answer is by forgiveness from wrong thoughts and actions. By changing thoughts from impure to wholesome thinking and by filling the mind with faith, you can experience a truly marvelous brain and soul washing.

The ugliness of hate is washed from the mind; all sins are forgiven. The inner cleanness thus gained is an amazing source of high spirits. Let us lighten up and remember:

- God forgave our sins . . .even the really bad ones
- We might as well forgive, because the offenses will never stop
- Vengeance is God's
- We must forgive ourselves
- Forgiveness leads to freedom

Lord thank you for the power to forgive.

---

[113] https://www.blueletterbible.org/kjv/

Days 264-265-266-267: Power to Receive the Covenant

Now the God of peace, that brought again from the dead our Lord Jesus, that great shepherd of the sheep, through the blood of the everlasting covenant.
- Hebrew 13:20 (KJV)[114]

For anyone who wishes to enjoy life and experience God's goodness, that is to be happy, respected, and in short, live a full, rich life, first Peter states, "He who would love life and see good days, let him refrain his tongue from evil, and his lips from speaking deceit. Let him turn away from evil and do good; Let him seek peace and pursue it."

In the two verses, above are listed just a few things that helps you receive the promised covenant of God. We are told to stop our tongues from speaking evil about anyone. Simply never say anything to hurt anyone. Moreover, we are to refrain from double talk, from shrewd remarks that are designed to advance our interests at someone else's disadvantage. We are to turn our back upon evil and in every way possible, do good. We are to help people and bring blessings into their lives.

Lord, help me to do the simple, honest Christian things to receive the covenant-life more abundantly!

Days 268-269-270-271: Power to See God

And Moses took the blood, and sprinkled it on the people ...And upon the nobles of the

---

[114] https://www.blueletterbible.org/kjv/

children of Israel he laid not his hand: also
they saw God, and did eat and drink.
- Exodus 24:8-11 (KJV)[115]

A physician once said that a large percent of patients did not need medicine; they needed God. To know God is to live. How do you find God?

Jeremiah said, "And you will seek me and find me, when you search for me with all your heart". The Holy Spirit is the power source of the Christian life. The Holy Spirit:

- Is God
- Came to dwell in you
- Came to convict the world of sin and justice
- Came to lead you in to the truth
- Came to glorify Christ
- Confirms your relationship with God

Say these words over and over until your mind deeply accepts the fact that God will come into your life when you want him with all your heart. Show me a person who knows God and I will show you a happy, enthusiastic and vital individual.

Days 272-273-274-275: Power to be Justified

Much more then, being now justified by His blood,
we shall be saved from wrath through him.
- Romans 5:9 (KJV)[116]

---

[115] https://www.blueletterbible.org/kjv/
[116] https://www.blueletterbible.org/kjv/

To be justified means to be vindicated, right, or acceptable. Jesus going to the cross and shedding his blood has made us in right standing with God. It is nothing that we have earned or could have done ourselves. With this being the case we need to:

- Practice kindly affection.
- Always take a generous, patient attitude.
- Practice consideration.
- Put the other person ahead of yourself.

Be Kind, Let Them In!

Ever came to a crossing in the parking lot, and people wanted to pass by. Did you let them in? Ever been in the line at the grocery store with a shopping cart full and someone came up with two items in their hand. Did you let them in?

Courtesy has amazing power to dissipate ill will. Free your heart of jealousy and resentment. The love you give will return to you, and your spirit will be lifted to new levels.

Days 276-277-278-279: Power to Have Peace that Passes Understanding

And the peace of God, which passeth all understanding, shall keep your hearts and minds through Christ Jesus.
-Philippians 4:7 (KJV)[117]

---

[117] https://www.blueletterbible.org/kjv/phl/4/7/s_1107007

Many times we will take one verse of scripture and make it our foundation to stand on without looking at the context within which that scripture is found. For example, if you would take a look at verse 6 of today's text, you will find the condition of this promise which tells us that God's peace is promised to keep those who pray, with thanksgiving, about everything. This is the kind of peace that human reasoning is incapable of fully understanding.

In today's society, it is supernatural to place your full confidence in God and be thankful 'in' every circumstance. Many times believers misquote or misunderstand the scriptures to say be thankful '**for**' everything. The faithful believer's heart and mind is guarded by this inner calm, in spite of the storm raging without.

To revitalize the spirit is a necessity, and this need is met by an amazing formula. Every longing of the human spirit finds enduring satisfaction in the life-giving message of Jesus—the Prince of Peace. It will remain a mystery, even to some believers, how a person can be so serene in the midst of turmoil.

This message becomes a perpetual well of self-renewing inspiration. From the water of life, our spirit is endowed with continuous refreshment and peace. A peace that pass all understanding.

Lord, thank you for allowing me to take my eyes off of circumstances and problems and receive peace.

Days 280-281-282-283: Power to Receive Healing

But He was wounded for our transgressions, He was bruised for our iniquities: the chastisement of our peace

was upon him; and with His stripes we are healed.
- Isaiah 53:5 (KJV)[118]

In maintaining your health, it is important to cultivate the attitude of spiritual surrender. Place yourself, your interest, hopes, purposes, finances, and health completely in God's hands

It's Already Done, Receive It!
We are Sunday school teachers at our local church. Nathaniel teaches the adolescence and I the adults.

Peter tells us to "cast all our care upon Him for He cares for us." If we surrender ourselves to the direction of God, being guided by His mighty hand, He will exalt us. He will help us attain our purposes and rise above all defeats. Cast all your care upon God.

Thank you for the promises of Proverb 3[119]. We can have a long healthy life with peace and health.

Days 284-285-286-287: Power to Receive Victory

And they overcame him (Satan) by the blood of
the Lamb and by the word of their testimony.
- Revelation 12:11 (KJV)[120]

---

[118] https://www.blueletterbible.org/kjv/
[119] https://www.blueletterbible.org/kjv/pro/3/8/t_conc_631008
[120] https://www.blueletterbible.org/kjv/

You have it in you to meet all your responsibilities. This consciousness contributes immeasurably to high spirits and happiness. It is difficult to face each day with a sense of inability and weakness. With such an attitude, life seems too much, and discouragement sets in.

Read Isaiah 41:10. Isaiah reminds us of God's promise to uphold us with His righteous right hand. This is a most important promise God makes to use. No matter how overwhelming your problems, you need have no fear. We have nothing to fear for God promise us the victory.

Receive this great fact. Hold this verse strongly in your consciousness until it sends its rugged courage throughout your entire life.

I got victory over the enemy and the world can't do me no harm.

Days 288-289-290-291: Power to be Sanctified

Wherefore Jesus also, that He might sanctify His people with His own blood, suffered without the gate.
- Hebrews 13:12 (KJV)[121]

What is sanctification? According to the thesauruses, sanctification is everything from beautification to hallowing. According to what I understand the Bible to say about sanctification, it is the renewing or your mind. Understanding the truth that is in the word of God and putting that truth into action in your life. This requires temperance which is the discipline to constantly put God's truth in your mind. To help you understand your own spiritual growth and how God's Word works in your life, John MacArthur[2] used three words

---

[121] https://www.blueletterbible.org/kjv/

to highlight steps in the sanctification process: Cognition, Conviction and Affection.

Cognition. One of the concepts of cognition is how you understand a matter—how you perceive a situation. Your thoughts and perceptions of God's Word sets the pattern for spiritual growth. Paul requested that we not only present our bodies to God but renew our minds;[122] in other words, our pattern of thinking. Cognition is understanding what the Bible says and what it means. Philip asked the eunuch did he understand what he was reading and the eunuch replied, how can I except some man should guide me?[123] The Word of God is true and once we get that understanding, you will be feel a sense of conviction.

Conviction. Conviction is having a strong belief or opinion. As you grow in your understanding of the Bible, you begin to develop convictions out of that understanding. Those convictions or beliefs determine how you live, or at least how you attempt to live. As God's truth takes over your mind, it produces principles that you do not desire to violate. That's sanctification—it's the transformation of your heart and will that compel you to obey God's Word. The third step in the biblical process of sanctification is:

Affection. Affection is defined as loving, caring, and regarding just to name a few. This affection for the truth of God's word can be described like that of your first love. It is not an infatuation, but a love that stems from a need like taking a breath of fresh air. A love that convicts you to hold to the truth of the word even when it hurts the flesh. Thank you for the power to be sanctified.

---

[122] https://www.blueletterbible.org/kjv/Romans 12:1-2

[123] https://www.blueletterbible.org/kjv/Acts 8:31

Ever heard the saying or the song, "Saved! Sanctified! Holy Ghost filled! Fire baptized! I got Jesus on the inside! And I running for my life!"? Ephesians 5:26[124] speaking of Jesus love and saving of us as "that he may sanctify and cleanse it (the church, us) with the washing of the water by the word."

Days 292-293-294-295: Power to Have a Clear Conscience

How much more shall the blood of Christ, Who through the Eternal Spirit offered himself without spot to God, purge your conscience (mind) from dead works, to serve the Living God? - Hebrews 9:14 (KJV)[125]

A guilty conscience is one of the worst of all depressants of the spirit. A prolonged, high-tempo pattern of thinking and living draws energy, leaving the spirit exhausted and dull. Therefore, the mind needs to experience a depth of quietness in which guilt will subside. Psalm tells us to be still and know that God is God.

Having attained and attitude of stillness, you will find the greatest of all thoughts will then come into your mind. You are then ready to know that "I am God". You realize that you cannot do everything, and the world does not rest on your shoulders.

The simple truth that you are to do your best and leave the rest to God comes back to your consciousness.

---

[124] https://www.blueletterbible.org/kjv/Ephesians 5:26
[125] https://www.blueletterbible.org/kjv/

Lord keep my mind from wandering to circumstances and challenges that I can give to you.

Days 296-297-298-299: Power to Remove Anger

A soft answer turns away wrath, but
a harsh word stirs up anger
- Proverbs 13:1 (KJV)[126]

Anger, what is it? Have you ever been sitting at a stop light, the light turns green, and before you can press on the accelerator, the person behind you starts angrily blowing the horn? Have you ever been given a fist and a middle finger because you were too slow in turning or changing lanes? If you have experienced either of the before mentioned, you have experienced anger in the form of road rage.

Anger is a strong emotion that you feel when you "think" someone has acted in a cruel, unfair, or unacceptable way. In return, this causes you to want to "fight back" or retaliate in some way. This type of anger is showing up in movie lines, grocery store lines, and definitely in the parking lots!

Protected from an Angry Beat Down!

One day as I was approaching a stop light, the light was caution in my direction, so I had planned to keep right through. The car coming through the light from my right came through at the same time. I slammed on the breaks and

---

[126] https://www.blueletterbible.org/kjv/

slid to a stop inches away from the car. The man jumped out of the driver's side of the car and came toward my car to jerk me out for a beat down.

He did not see my spouse who was retrieving fallen stuff in the floor. When my husband raised up and saw the man approaching me on the driver's side, he jumped out of the car and yelled, what are you doing?" The man ran back to his car cussing, jumped in and sped away. Thank, you Jesus!

Anger is a depressant of the spirit. So much energy is expended in anger that you are literally exhausted. The after effect is one of hopelessness, sadness or depression. Anger that simmers and seethes is even more depressing because it permits a constant leakage of energy. Any lingering anger or stress of this nature can make you physically ill or sick.

Fortunately, there is an effective method for correcting this condition. You will be amazed at the self-control it provides. The Holy Spirit dwelling within you can give you the power to overcome anger. You can cast your cares on Jesus because he cares for you. Get into a calm environment if possible and speak soothing truths from God's word like: I am the righteous of God in Christ Jesus. No weapon formed against me shall prosper.

Next time you feel anger arising, consider this: Jesus died for our sins. He sacrificed himself for our sins, so we could live. In that way we have been washed clean of sin in his blood and made holy.

Thank you, God, for allowing me to have power over anger.

Days 300-301-302-303: Power to be Redeemed

In whom we have redemption through His blood, even THE FORGIVENESS OF SINS, according to the riches of His grace.
- Ephesians 1:7 (KJV)[127]

Redemption is an important idea. According to the thesaurus, redemption is the same as recovery or reclaiming something or someone that was lost. Jesus redeemed us from the curse of the law[128].

Redemption came from the practices of ancient warfare. After a battle the victors would often capture some of the defeated. Among the defeated, the poorer ones would usually be sold as slaves, but the wealthy and important men, the men who mattered in their own country, would be held to ransom. When the people in their homeland had raised the required price, they would pay it to the victors and the captives would be set free. The process was called redemption, and the price was called the ransom.

To get a better understanding of redemption, when a slave had his freedom purchased, by a relative or by his own hard work and savings, he was redeemed. Sometimes the transaction took place at a temple, and a record was carved in the wall, so everyone would forever know that this former slave was now a redeemed, free man. Still another example of redemption is a man condemned to death might be set free by the paying of a price. Most importantly, Jesus bought us out of defeat, out of slavery, and out of a death sentence to reign as kings and priests with him forever.

How did Jesus do it? How did He pay a price to rescue us? Having become a curse for us means that Jesus became cursed

---

[127] https://www.blueletterbible.org/kjv/
[128] https://www.blueletterbible.org/kjv/gal/3/13/s_1094013

on our behalf; He stood in our place and took the curse we deserved.

Days 304-305-306-307: Power to be Liberated

Forasmuch as ye know that ye were not redeemed with corruptible things, as silver and gold, from your vain conversation received by tradition from your fathers; But with the precious blood of Christ, as of a lamb without blemish and without spot:
- I Peter 1:18-19 (KJV)[129]

We are good at telling people what they need to become spiritually alive. We even tell them that when Jesus died on the cross, He became a curse and because He was cursed, we're not cursed anymore. Many scriptures refer to Jesus as being our substitute. He carried the curse on the cross, so we wouldn't have to. Jesus paid the price to break the entire curse of the law, which included poverty, sickness, and spiritual death. The curse of the law had three basic divisions. The complete curse:

- Spiritual death
- Sickness and disease
- Poverty

The redemption:

- Eternal life
- Health and healing
- Prosperity

---

[129] https://www.blueletterbible.org/kjv/

Redeemed means to purchase back: to ransom; to liberate or rescue from captivity or bondage. Thank you, Jesus!

Days 308-309-310-311-312: Power to be Cleaned

But if we walk in the light, as He is in the light, we have fellowship one with another, And the blood of Jesus Christ His Son cleanseth us from all sins.
- I John 1:7 (KJV)[130]

Are you dirty? Any professing Christian would be very offended to be called dirty. However, scriptures refer to the everyday actions of many none believers as filthy.

- Filthy communication coming out of our mouths
- Our righteousness's is as filthy rags
- Filthy garments
- Filthy dreamers
- Filthy conversation of the wicked
- Teaching for filthy lucre's sake[131]

By trusting God to cleanse you with His radiant Light, you don't have to worry about not being clean enough to draw near. The washing of God is real. Thank him until you find freedom to believe that His Light is burning away any reason to feel dirty before him. To put on Light implies a promise that wearing His Light is realistic, and right, for all of us. However, since we receive the Holy Spirit by

---

[130] https://www.blueletterbible.org/kjv/
[131] https://www.blueletterbible.org/search/search.cfm?Criteria=filthy&t=KJV#s=s_primary_0_1

faith, walking in the light requires that we believe Jesus is a fountain of Light.

Days 313-314-315-316-317:
Power over Sin & Sinning

And from Jesus Christ, Who is the faithful witness, and the first begotten of the dead, and the Prince of the kings of the earth. Unto him that loved us, and washed us from our sins in His own blood.
- Revelation 1:5 (KJV)[132]

In Matthew 9 and verse 2, The Lord speaks and says, "Thy sins be forgiven thee." The beauty of this truth is Jesus' power over sin. Let's look at it with just a basic question: What is the most distinctive thing that Christianity must proclaim? You have already been given the answer. Clearly and unquestionably the most distinctive thing that Christianity should proclaim is the reality that sin can be forgiven.

The heart and the very lifeblood of the Christian message. Although the Christian faith has many values, many virtues, and has a myriad of endless applications, the core of all this is Christian believe the Apostles Creed. Briefly summed up say that:

Jesus was born through the Virgin Mary, that God the Father, Jesus Christ as the Son of God, and the Holy Spirit are One. The death, descent into hell, resurrection and ascension of Christ.[133]

The most essential message that God ever gave to man is that man, a sinner, can know the fullness of forgiveness for that

---

[132] https://www.blueletterbible.org/kjv/
[133] http://christianityinview.com/creeds.html

sin. That is the heart of the message of Christianity. Thank you, Jesus, for giving me the power to stop sinning.

Days 318-319-320-321-322:
Power to Be Justified

Much more then, being now justified by His blood,
we shall be saved from wrath through Him
- Romans 5:9 (KJV)

If Jesus Christ, in his endless comparison towards us gave his life for ours, while we were yet enemies; being now justified by his blood - by his death on the cross, and thus reconciled to God, we shall be saved from wrath - from punishment for past transgression, through him - by what he has thus suffered for us.

The enmity existing before rendered the reconciliation necessary. In every human heart, there is a measure of enmity to holiness, and, consequently to the author of it. Men seldom suspect this; for one property of sin is to blind the understanding, so that men do not know their own state.

Do you believe that Jesus died for our sins? With that said and believe that he rose again for our justification. His resurrection to life, is the grand proof that he has accomplished whatever he had purposed pertaining to the salvation of man.

Thank you, Jesus, for justifying me.

Days 323-324-325-326-327: Power
to Stay Under the Blood

For when Moses had spoken every precept to all the

> *people according to the law, he took the blood of calves*
> *and of goats, with alter, and scarlet wool, and hyssop,*
> *and sprinkled both the book, and all the people.*
> *- Hebrews 9:19 (KJV)*[134]

The shed blood of the burnt offerings was contained in a basin. Moses took some of this blood and poured part of it by the altar. Then he took a hyssop, dipped it in the basin and sprinkled the blood on the people sealing the agreement giving the Israelites full access to God, with joy.

Then Moses, Nadab, Abihu and he seventy elders went up to the mountain to meet God. The Lord appeared to them, coming down a sapphire-stone walk. These men saw a table spread before them and Scripture infers that with ease, comfort, and no fear of judgement, they sat in God's presence and ate and drank with him. Exodus 24:11 said that the nobles of the children of Israel ate and drank with God and God laid not His hands on them.

It is awesome that these men could eat and drink in the very presence of God when shortly before they had feared for their lives. They didn't fear! It was because the blood (a type and shadow of what Jesus' blood would do) had been sprinkled on them. They understood the safety, the power, the security in that! What about you today?

Days 328-329-330-331-332:
Power in the Shed Blood

> *And the blood shall be to you for a token upon the*
> *houses where ye are and when I see the blood, I will*

---

[134] https://www.blueletterbible.org/kjv/

pass over you, and the plague shall not be upon you
to destroy you, when I smite the land of Egypt
- Exodus 12:13 (KJV)[135]

This blood is a type of the blood of Christ. The blood that flowed at Calvary was not wasted. That precious blood was collected in a "heavenly fountain". There is a gospel song that says, "There is a fountain filled with blood and sinners plunged beneath that flow lose all their guilt and stain…" We may not plunge into the flow of blood, but we better have our heart sprinkled with it.

When Moses read the law to the people they said that they understood it and that they would obey it. Their agreement with this covenant was sealed or ratified with sacrificial blood. Hebrews 9:19 tells us that Moses "…took the blood… and sprinkled both the book and he people…"

On this occasion it had nothing to do with forgiveness and remission of sin, but with relationship. The sprinkling of the blood on the people sanctified them; it cleansed them and made them fit to be in God's presence. What about you? Have you allowed Jesus's blood the give you the power to be in fellowship with him? If not, do it today.

Days 333-334-335-336: Power to be Obedient

And they shall take of the blood, and strike it
on the two side posts and on the upper door post
of the houses, wherein they shall eat it.[136]

Obedience is an action, not a reaction. It is an exercise of

---

[135] https://www.blueletterbible.org/kjv/
[136] https://www.blueletterbible.org/kjv/

our wills. For example, we do not forgive only when we feel like it. We forgive when we are asked for forgiveness by others, or led to forgive by God. We don't have to feel like forgiving someone to forgive them. They probably didn't hurt us because they felt like it, and we don't have to feel like it to forgive them. If you believe in forgiveness, exercise your will in obedience to God and forgive.

In these days as the Lord is preparing us for a great outpouring of His presence, let us choose to put away disobedience and become fully obedient to the Lord in all things. We need to repent of any and every way we have allowed the spirit of Anti-Christ to work in our lives or through our lives affecting others. God wants the fire of His presence to be a blessing that empowers His Church, and He is calling us to embrace obedience not for His sake, but ours. We can walk in the freedom that obedience brings, not by striving to obey through legalism but because we have been so deeply loved and desire to display our love for the Lord through willing obedience. The Lord has a beautiful freedom for every believer if we will walk with him in the simplicity of obedience — an obedience that will invite His presence and release His power into and through our lives.

Days 337-338-339: Power to Bear Witness

This is that came by water and blood, even Jesus Christ not by water only, but by water and blood. And it is the Spirit that beareth witness, because the Spirit is truth.
-1 John 5:6 (KJV)[137]

When we bear witness, we lovingly give our attention to the other without judgment. We comfort without smothering.

---

[137] https://www.blueletterbible.org/kjv/

We play a supporting role, powerfully upholding another, who is starring his or her life. It is not about us. It is about them. Yet, we make a profound decision when we do not try to fix their pain and suffering or share in their experience by telling how we had a similar experience. Bearing witness says, "You are not alone. I see you. I witness what you are experiencing. What you are experiencing matters to me. I surround you with my love."

For those of you who struggle with going to see a sick or dying friend or relative because you just don't know what to say or do, try just showing up and bearing witness. Often, it is our own discomfort and the feeling of helplessness that we are avoiding by not going into these situations. Sometimes we forget that our job is not to fix the situation at hand, but rather to help lift the burden of the other person by letting them know we care enough to show up. In good times and in bad, in sickness and in health, it is important that we show up for each other.

Days 340-341-342: Power to Walk in the Light

But if we walk in the light, as he is in the light we have fellowship one with another, and the blood of Jesus Christ his Son cleanseth us from all sin.
- I John 1:7 (KJV)

What does it mean to walk in the light? As a girl at home we had to walk to get water by lantern light. My oldest brother would be in front leading the way down the path. We had to follow him with the light as he stayed in the path. Later, we moved up to using the flashlight, but the process was still the same-follow the one with the light and stay in the path.

Just as we followed the leader who had the light to get to the water in the spring, "walking in the Light" in the passage of scripture means to walk in a way that is consistent with the Holy Scriptures. Since Jesus is the light of the world[138], he tells us that if we walk in the light that we shall not walk in darkness but will have the light of life[139]. We will be able to live a pure and holy life separated from evil.

The good news is that as believers walking as Jesus did, we have received a new power over sin and have assurance of our salvation.

Jesus gave us an example as he went about doing the will of the Father. If you tell a person how to do something they may get somewhat of a concept in their mind, but if that same person can see an example or you doing it, they can follow the example much easier than just a verbal command.

Jesus is our example and so John points to Jesus as our example. And, first, He is our example in our relationship with God. "For if we walk in the light as He is in the light, then we have fellowship with God and the blood of Jesus Christ, His Son, is cleansing us from all sin.[140]"

So, Jesus is our light and example in our walk. John goes on to tell us in chapter 2, verse 6, "He that says that he abides in him ought himself also to walk even as He walked."[141] So again, Christ our example in our walk, our walk with God, our relationship with God.

The scriptures speak many times about our "walk". The Holy Ghost gives us the power to "walk" or "live" a holy,

[138] https://www.blueletterbible.org/John 9:5
[139] https://www.blueletterbible.org/John 8:12
[140] https://www.blueletterbible.org/kjv/1jo/1/7/s_1160007
[141] https://www.blueletterbible.org/kjvI John 2:6

sanctified life. Loving God and our fellowman the way Jesus did when he became flesh and dwelled among us giving us that much needed example. Thank you, Jesus!

Days 343-344-345-346: Power to Face Challenges

Wherefore Jesus also, that he might sanctify the people with this own blood suffered without the gate.
- Hebrew 13:12 (KJV)[142]

When big Spiritual challenges come your way, are you up to dealing with them? Or do you hope the challenge, the Issue, the Decision, the Person, and the Ministry will JUST go away

Christians today may want to RUN from the spiritual challenges that confront them. It's so important for you to learn early in life, NOT to RUN from challenges! Now there are some things you should run from. You should run from immorality! You should run from Temptation or someone who is trying to tempt you to sin. However, there are things that God has called believers to do and WE shouldn't run from our responsibility. Nehemiah teaches that Spiritual challenges:

- Calls for intense prayer
- A need to realize who God is
- Constant focused prayer
- Bold actions
- Depends completely on God

---

[142] https://www.blueletterbible.org/kjv/

- Requires the avoidance of distractions
- Requires the help of other saints
- Will Manifest God's power

Thank you, Jesus, for the power to face challenges.

Days 347-348-349-350: Power to be Bold

*Having therefore, brethren, boldness to enter
into the holiest by the blood of Jesus.
- Hebrew 10:19 (KJV)*[143]

Is there something you've been wanting or trying to do, but can't seem to get the courage up? Whether it's apologizing to a loved one after a long period of misunderstanding, or simply being friendly to a co-worker, stop thinking about acting and do something. Boldness is the opposite of hesitation. Whenever you're feeling hesitant in interactions with others, or in deciding for yourself, learn to swallow your pride and make the first move.

Ultimately, boldness must do with understanding your strengths and weaknesses, then moving beyond them. Don't try to hide your problems or failures, but accept them as part of you. If someone asks you to do something you don't want to do, refuse. Saying "No" will reinvigorate your individuality and help you to feel bold, ensuring that you're ready and willing to go out and get what you want. Don't feel like you should make up an excuse or explanation. People must learn to respect your honesty and boldness

It's not enough to simply say you're going to do something, you should do it, or people think of you as a flake. When your

---

[143] https://www.blueletterbible.org/kjv/

word is good, and you follow through with actions, people will trust you and look upon you as a bold, reliable, complicated person

Days 351-352-353-354: Power to Discern

And Jesus answered and said unto him, Blessed art thou, Simon Barjona for flesh and blood hath not revealed it unto thee, but my Father which is in heaven.
- Matthew 16:17 (KJV)[144]

To discern is to see or understand the difference; to make distinction; as, to discern between good and evil, truth and falsehood. There are some things that differ one from other; as morality and grace, earthly things, and heavenly things, carnal and spiritual, temporal and eternal things, law and Gospel, the doctrines of men, and the doctrines of Christ; all which differ as much as chaff and wheat, as gold, silver, precious stones, and wood, hay, stubble.

These are to be tried and proved; they are not to be received without distinction, but should be examined, which is right and best to be chosen and preferred; and to such trial and examination it is necessary that a man should be transformed, by the renewing of his mind, that he should have spiritual light, knowledge, and experience, have his spiritual senses exercised to discern the difference of things, and the guidance, direction, and influence of the Spirit of God.

Discerning must be made according to the word of God, the Scriptures of truth, in the light of the divine Spirit, and with spiritual judgment and sense. Search the scriptures and some things will be found excellent, as Christ, and the knowledge of him in his person, offices, grace, righteousness, blood, sacrifice,

---

[144] https://www.blueletterbible.org/kjv/

and satisfaction, and the several truths of the Gospel relating to peace, pardon, justification, adoption, sanctification, and eternal life; and of the several doctrines of the Gospel

Days 355-356-357-358: Power to be Faithful

And from Jesus Christ, who is the faithful witness, and the first begotten of the dead, and the prince of the kings of the earth. Unto him that loved us, and washed us from our sins in his own blood.
-Revelation 1:5 (KJV) [145]

Be faithful to God for He is faithful to you. Psalms states, "For He shall give His angels charge over you to keep you in all your ways.

How your spirit will rise as the amazing truth grips you that nothing in this world can hurt you. God is watching over you to keep you in all your ways. His amazing kindness and faithfulness surrounds you always. You go through life with a high-hearted spirit, knowing God is faithful.

You are called to have the fruit of being faithful in the little things. If your talent is music, then be faithful to sing around the house to your kids. If your calling is to communicate then make videos using available media to share with your family and friends. If you have the gifts of helps, then find your friends and neighbors and help them. Stay connected to the Vine, Jesus, and He will grow faithfulness in your life. He will enable you to be faithful in the little things.

Thank you for your faithfulness.

---

[145] https://www.blueletterbible.org/kjv/

Days 359-360-361-362: Power in Being Born Again

And I saw the woman drunken with the blood of the saints, and with the blood of the martyrs of Jesus, and when I saw her, I wondered with great admiration - Revelation 17:6 (KJV)[146]

"The great prostitute described in these verses is a portrayal of Apostate Christendom in the end time. When the Lord comes for his saints, all true believers were caught up to be with the Lord, but left behind were many thousands of those who made some profession of faith in Christ and claimed to be Christians who were not born again. These constituted the apostate Church which will dominate the scene politically and religiously up to the midpoint of that last seven years before the Second Coming.

The apostasy, called adultery and fornication, of course refers to spiritual unfaithfulness, not to physical adultery. The church, devoid of any redeeming influence, is now completely united with the world, and, as the passage indicates, is working hand in glove with the political powers.

Let us pray that we are truly born again! The new birth is more than an initial reformation of life. It is the long-term commitment after baptism. It is the maintenance of life with God through Christ. It is to "continue with the Lord". The new birth is the start. After being born of water and the Spirit, there is an ongoing future life of righteousness to be maintained and grown

---

[146] https://www.blueletterbible.org/kjv/

Days 363-364-365 (366 If Leap Year): Power in the Blood of Jesus

Likewise also the cup after supper, saying, this cup is the New Testament in my blood, which is shed for you. - Luke 22:20 (KJV)[147]

What do you know about the blood Jesus shed? Christians often sing about the power of the blood. One of my favorite songs is "Power, power, wonder-working power in the precious blood of the Lamb"! But most believers seldom enter the power of that blood.

We constantly "plead the blood" as magic formula of protection. We do not comprehend the great significance of the blood. Few can explain its great glory and benefits. We observe Jesus' shed blood sacrifice every time we take communion.

Remember in Exodus 12 when the Israelites were commanded to take a bunch of hyssop, dip it in the blood of a slain lamb and sprinkle it onto the lintel and two side-posts of their front door? Well if Christ is Lord of your life, then your door posts "your heart" have been sprinkled by His blood for forgiveness AND for protection!

Jesus' blood totally protects you against all the destroying powers of Satan. When the enemy encounters, a heart covered by the Blood, he must pass over you. They cannot touch you because they cannot touch anyone sprinkled with the Blood— the Blood that is waiting to be sprinkled on the door posts of hearts around the world!

---

[147] https://www.blueletterbible.org/kjv/luk/22/20/s_995020

For ALL the Days of Your Life

Dedicate Time to the Word of God. Set aside a specific amount of time to study the word of God every day. Keep a praise in your mouth and meditate on him during your daily activities. Stay amazed and the "little things".

References

The **Authorized Version** or **King James Version (KJV)**, 1611, 1769. All scripture quotations are taken from the Kings James Version unless otherwise noted

Outside of the United Kingdom, the KJV is in the public domain. Within the United Kingdom, the rights to the KJV are vested in the Crown

The King James Version of the Bible was originally published in 1611.

Scripture notation marked NIV are taken from the Holy Bible New International Version© NIV® Copyright © 1973, 1978, 1984, International Bible Society.

Has This Book Impacted Your Walk with God?

Deacon Nathaniel and Evangelist Dr. Janie Torain would love to hear your testimony. Please let them know if **Power 365** has had an effect in your life or in the lives of your love ones.

Send your email to mstoe29@msn.com or n_torain@hotmail.com.

Like us on Facebook www.facebook.com/janie.sheeleytorain

About the Author

The author is a retired high school teacher and a retired community college adult basic skills online facilitator. She has a doctorate degree in educational leadership. A specialist degree in curriculum and instruction, a master's in Education Technology, and a bachelor's degree in comprehensive Business Education. She is also a National Board-certified teacher in Career and Technical Education. She serves her local church and community as an usher, choir member, and Evangelist and Sunday school teacher.

She has previously published her dissertation research, *Virtual Learning: Is It Conducive to Student Achievement*, and her master thesis, *An Assessment of the Impact of Technology on the Performance of Exceptional Children in Computer Adaptive*

Testing in Person County. She has also written one children's book, *If I Could Quit School for a Day*. She and her husband, had 7 children, 24 grandchildren and 3 great grandchildren and live in Roxboro, North Carolina.

The Fire is Burning

The success of being a first-generation high school and community college graduate, really stirred up the fire for lifelong learning. She continues to seek God for guidance on how to go in and out among his people. God has given her a special love for teenagers and young adults.

God is a Keeper

On November 15, 2013, the sudden death of the youngest daughter left her to raise two of her grandchildren who are now pre=teen and a teenager. Life is Good!

The Favor of God

In 2008, she was ordained an evangelist at her church where she faithfully serve as Sunday school teacher, choir member, usher, and preach second Sundays. She and her husband spend any "free time" advising the 6 children on how to raise the 22 grandchildren and three great grandchildren. God has blessed them to become the parents of their baby girl's two children, making the total grandchildren, 24. Their daughter went to be with the Lord at the young age of 33. They now are blessed to go to kick-ball, basketball, and football games, karate practice, and the list goes on!

LIFE IS GOOD!

~Joshua 24:15~

"For God has not given us the spirit of fear but of POWER, and of love and of a sound mind"

II Timothy 1:7

This inspiring prayer guide is perfect to keep with you everywhere you travel for moments when you need a little boost of power. Packed with more than 365 scriptural references, testimonies, and encouragement, this collection will help you follow Jesus as he lead you through the everyday joys and challenges of your calling every day of the year.

Endnotes

1   Moody, Steve. God is Love-Life, Hope & Truth Retrieved
     September 18, 2018 from https://lifehopeandtruth.com/god/who-
     is-god/god-is-love/

2   MacArthur, John. (2012) Grace to you: Unleashing God's Truth
     One Verse at a Time. Retrieved August 16, 2018 from .https://
     goo.gl/7Pp4id

Printed in the United States
By Bookmasters